Working with Black Youth

Opportunities for Christian Ministry

EDITED BY

Charles R. Foster
and Grant S. Shockley

ABINGDON PRESS
Nashville

WORKING WITH BLACK YOUTH:
OPPORTUNITIES FOR CHRISTIAN MINISTRY

Edited by Charles R. Foster, Grant S. Shockley.

Copyright © 1989 by Abingdon Press

Library of Congress Cataloging-in-Publication Data

Working with Black Youth: opportunities for ministry / [edited by] Charles R. Foster, Grant S. Shockley.
      p. cm.
Bibliography: p.
ISBN 0-687-46196-0 (alk. paper)
1. Church work with Afro-American youth.
I. Foster, Charles R., 1937-
II. Shockley, Grant S., 1919-
BV4468.2.A34W67 1989
261.8'34235'08996073—dc20

              89-7021
              CIP

This book is printed on acid-free paper.

MANUFACTURED BY THE PARTHENON PRESS AT
NASHVILLE, TENNESSEE, UNITED STATES OF AMERICA

CONTENTS

FOREWORD

*T*he idea for this book originated in a series of conversations among eleven professors of religious education. We participated in a seminar that met twice a year over four years to explore ways to strengthen theological education in the area of youth ministry. We were part of a special project on "Youth Ministry and Theological Education" sponsored by the Lilly Foundation and conducted under the leadership of Dr. Sara Little of Union Theological Seminary in Richmond, Virginia. During our sessions together, seminar members shared course syllabi and bibliographies, identified issues for investigation, conversed with people involved in various forms of youth ministry, engaged in focused research, and presented papers for discussion. *Working with Black Youth* is the culmination of continuing discussions of our seminar group. It began in 1985 as we became increasingly aware of the lack of attention given by the church and theological schools to the experience of ethnic youth in general and of African American youth in particular in their courses of study. We also discovered limited literature on the subject. Notable exceptions included Caesar D. Coleman's essay on "Why Should We Evangelize Black Youth" in the September-October, 1969 issue of *Religious*

Education and the 1971 Krishheim Report on "Youth and the Black Church" also published in *Religious Education.*

A survey of denominational literature and policy revealed a similar lack of attention to the character of African American youth culture, the experience of African American youth in the church, and the relevance of existing approaches in the church's ministries to and with African American youth. We discovered that most of the assumptions informing ministries with African American youth had been drawn from the experiences of predominantly white churches. We wrote this book, consequently, to begin to address this void in the literature.

Our intention has been to establish not a program guide or handbook, but *a beginning theoretical framework for black youth ministries,* by drawing from studies of black youth experiences in the church and in the larger national culture, and the resources of black theology. We have identified basic assumptions and guiding principles that could be the impetus for pastors, teachers and youth leaders, curriculum editors and writers, denominational youth staff, seminary professors, and students to develop appropriate programmatic structures for black youth ministry.

A mini-grant from the Youth Ministry and Theological Schools Education Project made it possible to invite three prominent young black scholars—Janice Hale-Benson from Cleveland State University, Jacquelyn Grant from the Interdenominational Theological Center, and Romney Moseley from Candler School of Theology at Emory University—to provide leadership for a consultation on Black Youth Ministry in November, 1987. Under the auspices of the Multicultural Resources Center of the Scarritt Graduate School and the National Council of the Churches of Christ in the United States of America, the consultation included sixty church leaders representing eleven denominations involved in local, regional, and national ministries with black youth. The discussion of the three papers by Hale-Benson, Grant, and Moseley by the consultation participants provided the agenda for the introductory and concluding chapters of this book. We are indebted to the consultation participants for many of the themes and ideas in these two chapters. At the same time we assume full responsibilty for their content and organization.

We are grateful to Robert W. Lynn and the Lilly Foundation for their awareness of the need for concentrated attention by theological schools to youth ministry issues. We appreciate the continuing encouragement and support given by Sara Little, the director of the project and the leader of our seminar discussions; the members of the project steering committee: Daniel Aleshire, Craig Dykstra, and Paul Nichols; and our colleagues of the Richmond seminar on the Youth Ministry and Theological Education Project: Janet Fishburn, Freda Gardner, Margaret Krych, Robin Maas, John Nelson, Rick Osmer, Robert Poerschke, and Ed Trimmer. The timely advice and suggestions given by Dr. Nichols, our planning consultant, repeatedly proved to be valuable. We also wish to acknowledge the enthusiastic assistance and help we received from the members of the Advisory Board of the Multicultural Resources Center and the administration and staff of the Scarritt Graduate School in planning and conducting the consultation on black youth ministries. We are especially grateful to the writers of the three papers and the participants in the consultation whose commitment to the task and sensitivity to the issues inspired us to expand our conversation to the church at large. And we are indebted to Brenda Stevenson and

Doris Shockley for their persistent and attentive assistance in preparing the manuscript for publication.

Charles R. Foster
Grant S. Shockley

Chapter One

Historical Perspectives

GRANT S. SHOCKLEY

*T*he evolution of the contemporary crisis in Christian youth education in the black church can best be understood by following it in the context of the church's rise. There are two reasons for this approach. First, the black church is the matrix from which the religious experiences of black people emerged. Second, the religious developments, cultural changes and social forces which influenced the black church are precisely those which impacted the black experience and affected black youth. This introduction then will briefly explore the major developmental periods in American black church history to understand the religious, social, and educational issues that were and are involved in ministering with black youth through the churches.

Black Folk Religion

African Americans were brought to North America in the early seventeenth century. They came as captives, not as settlers. Their lot was to be in "perpetual servitude." Relatively few obtained their freedom until emancipation in 1863. Their religions were basically African in origin with some Roman Catholic or Islamic influence. A composite of the religious beliefs of the early African American slave probably included a high god concept, ancestor worship, and magic. This amalgam of beliefs came into contact with Christianity in its various expressions in colonial America. Thus, African religious influences, the slave and "free" black experience, and early American Christianity became the essence of the content of black folk religion in pre-emancipation American history.[1]

During the pre-emancipation period, this early "folk religion" informed the content and style of Christian education in black churches, families, and communities especially in the South. Several strategies structured the educational experience in both South and North. The most prominent for youth were the Sunday schools or variations of them. In the South a few black churches had Sunday schools with a class (or classes) for youth. In other churches religious instruction was provided for youth in groups similar to Sunday school classes. Most were conducted on an oral instruction basis. In contrast northern Sunday schools often tended to be privately sponsored for black children and youth or related to one of the black Methodist or Baptist denominations. Although difficult to document, a number of more informal sources of education for youth in this period included quiet times with families, stories from grandparents in extended families, celebrations based on African folklore and Bible reading.[2] Finally "Free African Societies," functioning as mutual aid and support communities, existed in many northern cities to foster high moral character and assist members and families in times of need. In retrospect, their members and leaders served admirably as role models for black children and youth.

Black Youth, Black Church,
and the Post Civil War Years

After the Civil War the black church experienced a period of phenomenal growth and expansion. Baptists, building on foundations laid earlier, established congregations throughout the South. During the 1870s thousands of black Methodists withdrew from the Methodist Episcopal Church, South, and organized the Christian Methodist Episcopal Church. This development together with the evangelistic efforts of the African Methodist Episcopal Church (AME) and the African Methodist Episcopal Zion Church (AMEZ) netted tens of thousands of members including thousands of youth. Somewhat later (1880) the black National Baptists created their first national body. By 1916 in fact, more than 90% of all black Christians in the nation belonged to one of the seven nation-wide black denominations. The remaining 10% were members of black local churches related to predominantly white national church bodies. At the time only 300,000 blacks considered themselves Roman Catholic. This number has since increased to more than one million. Although the fastest growing black church now, at that time the Pentecostal Church of God in Christ had only a fraction of its present multi-million membership.

Several things were happening in the work of churches among youth during these post-Civil war years. The Sunday school, initiated by independent black churches and denominations, remained the principal source of formal Christian education among black youth. The energy and funds from white educational missions during this period were usually channeled into developing schools for ex-slaves for rudimentary instruction. Some of these schools eventually became the founding units for most of today's black church-related colleges.

The Christian Endeavor Movement, organized in 1881 by Francis E. Clark in a Portland, Maine Congregational church, became the model for the formal organization of youth work in black churches and denominations. In some respects an outgrowth of the Sunday school, Christian Endeavor society membership requirements for youth usually between 10 and 18 years of age meant commitment, constancy, faithful attendance, and serious Bible study and prayer.[3] The random formation of Christian Endeavor societies began soon after their founding in African Methodist Episcopal churches in the early 1880s and among black Baptists later in that same decade. By 1893, H. R. Stitt had organized the Christian Endeavor Society in the African Methodist Episcopal Church as well.[4]

The Christian Endeavor society was "adapted and adopted" by the churches for almost a decade.[5] With the 1889 merger of Methodist Episcopal Church youth groups and societies of various names, however, the Christian Endeavor dominance of Protestant youth ministry ended. This emerging denominational emphasis took hold in black churches at the same time. As early as 1885 black National Baptists allied their Christian Endeavor societies with the Baptist Young People's Union of the Southern Baptist convention. In the AMEZ Church in 1896, the Christian Endeavor Society became the Varick Christian Endeavor Society, honoring the founder and first bishop of the denomination, James Varick (1750-1827). The Christian Methodist Episcopal Church authorized the organization of an Epworth League in 1892 which became operative in 1898. The AME Church changed the name of its youth societies in 1907 to the Allen Christian Endeavor Societies to similarly honor its founder, Richard Allen (1760-1831).[6]

Christian education programs generally and youth programs specifically were influenced by white Protestant church models. These approaches tended to be inadequate in meeting the religious needs of the majority of black church youth. They have also proven to be inadequate in responding to the recent voracious changes in black churches and communities.[7]

Black Youth and Black Church
Before the Black Revolution

At least three social forces influenced the response of the black church to the precarious situation in black youth ministry during the first half of the present century. First, from the late Reconstruction Period in the 1880s until the 1920s, large numbers of black people including youth, migrated to urban areas in the north and west seeking employment or better opportunities for themselves and their families. Uprooted, unskilled, and barely literate, many of them became marginalized persons in the highly impersonal life of the city. The once-effective "mutual aid" societies, used by black churches to orient newcomers were inadequate to care for the masses of blacks who kept pouring into metropolitan centers.

Sociologist E. Franklin Frazier has observed that this migration created several problems for black churches and communities: the difficulty of finding housing for migrating families, the loss of disciplinary control by working mothers, marital separations, and youth involvement in delinquent behavior and crime.[8]

Urbanization not only contributed to the breakdown of important structures and controls in many families, it often stratified the black community socio-economically. Education, occupation, and income divided communities and sometimes families roughly into upper, lower, and middle classes.[9]   This new situation had important implications for black churches. With some exceptions, black churches had previously been classless institutions. Given stratification however, black sociologists have agreed with Frazier's conclusion that "the Negro church...[adapted]...itself to the general outlook and religious requirements of the different classes.   In effect many working and middle class black people preferred the Baptist or (African) Methodist churches, while significant numbers of professional and affluent blacks often held membership in congregations related to predominantly white (Protestant or Catholic) denominations."[10] Interpreters of the history and sociology of black church institutions and behavior are fairly agreed that storefront churches arose in part to accommodate the social and religious needs of those black immigrants who failed either to find a black congregation or to find acceptance in one or another of the established black churches.

The stratification of black churches also contributed to the formation of the "institutional church." A number of black denominations in northern and midwestern cities developed all-purpose programs and facility churches to meet the needs of the increasing numbers of migrating blacks.   Congregations bought or built churches with gymnasiums and fellowship halls, in part to house the recreation programs initiated for youth. Carter G. Woodson points out that AME pastor Dr. Reverdy C. Ransom started the first institutional-type church in Chicago during the early 1900s.[11] The accommodation of the black church to the needs of these new arrivals illustrates the fact that black churches realized they existed to meet the needs of people. At the same time, the accommodation tended to reinforce emerging socio-economic class distinctions in the black community. This exclusiveness, where it existed, became especially evident to youth and may account for the general decline in youth attendance or participation in the youth programs of many prestigious black churches in this period.

Class and color were not the only factors that created tension in black churches as they sought to meet the spiritual needs of their members and the community. A more formidable adversary was what Frazier called "secularization," a point of view that regarded the human condition in this world as important and the moderate enjoyment of worldly pleasures as normal. Dr. Lawrence N. Jones, Dean of the Howard University Divinity School has emphasized this same point in his observation that "the migration of blacks from the farms to the cities has been the most significant phenomenon affecting the churches in this century....This generation is much more secularized in outlook and much more aware of the ways in which black peoples' lives are shaped by structures and institutions they do not control."[12]

The church's response to youth needs involved in the migrations of rural southern blacks, the increasing stratification of the black community and church, and the pervasive influence of secularization from the beginning of the century to the beginning of the Freedom Decade (1955) tended to be mixed and modest. The concern of black church and community leaders for black youth is revealed more in conference reports and research studies that focused on black youth than in the church's programmatic response. The history of the black youth experience and the research on black youth during the first half of the century however, has been hidden in journals and libraries. An adequate understanding of the contemporary crisis in the church's ministry to black youth depends upon retrieving something of this hidden story.

The first book to recognize the problems of black youth and the status of youth work in black churches was *The United Negro: His Problems and Progress*, edited by D. Garland Penn and J. W. E. Bowen and published in 1902. It reported the findings of the Negro Young People's Christian and Educational Congress called by a distinguished group of young black leaders and held in Atlanta, Georgia earlier that year. This first-of-its-kind gathering of Christian leaders in religion, education, and social work proposed a united approach to the amelioration of the deplorable condition of black people and especially of youth. Its conclusions were intended to be implemented by "homes, firesides, churches, Sunday schools, young people's societies...."[13]

The first scientific survey of Christian education among black youth in the United States was carried out by Harvard trained W.E.B. DuBois, the nation's first black social scientist. This study was a component of the first major empirical study of *The Negro Church* in 1903. This unique phenomenological study asked children and youth to describe their perceptions of such things as the Christian faith, the church, the meaning of their faith. DuBois, anticipating the work of recent developmental psychologists, discovered that children tended to express their faith more in concrete terms than youth who tended to understand religion in reference to a "higher will."[14]

Other studies focused on the church's role and function in the lives of black youth. In *Morals and Manners Among Negro Americans* for example, DuBois observed in

1919 that "The young people's societies" in black churches
"are largely literary in their nature and the Sunday school
perfunctory." In 1931 a society of black Yale Divinity
School students sponsored a conference to help "produce a new type of leadership, one which will give
itself...to the creation of a new social order based upon
the principles of Jesus Christ." During this conference
George E. Haynes of the Federal Council of Churches observed that "the Negro Church...is largely an adult organization. It does not provide an adequate outlet for youth
and children. Many Negro churches still cling to the idea
that the child before the threshold of puberty is not
competent to experience the new birth."[15] From the
beginning of the century, this theme is repeated through
the literature for several decades.

   The Negro's Church, the first social analysis of youth work
in the black church by B. E. Mays and J. W. Nicholson,
reinforces this negative view of the youth's role. From
their survey, they discovered that youth groups and Sunday schools were the major Christian education activities
in black churches. They suggested that the effectiveness
of the youth groups were limited however, because they
1) lacked clear, intentional purposes; 2) had low enroll-
ments and poor attendance; 3) lacked youth participation in planning; 4) were poorly guided; 5) were mostly
limited to the youth of church families, and 6) had little
community outreach.[16]

   Mays and Nicholson's work sets the tone for subsequent studies into the relationship of black youth to the
church up to the Civil Rights era. The emphasis upon
youth participation and attitudes toward the church
tended to dominate their attention. These two concerns
may be observed in the research reports of Charles H.
Wesley and William E. Carrington. In his 1936 study,

"The Religious Attitudes of Negro Youth," Wesley reports
that

1. many attended church services because they "like"
   them;
2. some attended because there was no where else to go;
3. the majority attended because of parental influence;
4. black church youth tended to be religiously conservative;
5. few preferred the ministry as a profession; and
6. youth universally demanded a more practical Christianity.

Carrington on the other hand, in "Negro Youth and
the Religious Education Program of the Church," assessed the structure of black Christian youth education
during the 1920s and 1930s. He discovered that church
programs for black youth tended to

1. be "the second most important division of the church;"
2. be branches of adult controlled organizations sometimes giving rise to a "radical left-wing" group of youth
   seeking self-determination;
3. involve a trend toward cooperation with community-
   based character building organizations, such as Boy
   and Girl Scouts;
4. construe recreation for youth in narrowly defined terms;
5. imitate adult church activity with little youth creativity;
6. be guided by poorly trained adult leaders; and
7. lack youth-oriented management methods. In 1935
   John Dillingham further observed that the intermedi-
   ate departments of 10-to-16-year-olds in most churches
   separated the boys from the girls.[17]

This picture of church approaches to black youth is expanded by another genre of research during the 1940s
which focused on the social contexts rather than the

programmatic life of black youth in the church. The American Youth Council, established in 1935 by the American Council on Education, oversaw a series of studies mandated to consider "all the needs of [black] youth and appraise the facilities and resources for serving those needs."[18] The research of the council consequently focused in part upon the black church.

Ira D. Reid's *In a Minor Key: Negro Youth in Story and Fact* introduced the series. In a summary of previous studies on the role of black churches in youth ministry since 1900, Reid made four noteworthy observations: 1) in the black community the black church's role changed from one of centrality to marginality; 2) the shape of the black church reflected a broadening spectrum of beliefs and options; 3) the once family constituency base of the black church now shared its ministry with the efforts of other community organizations, evangelists, and the media; 4) black youth, once content with the narrower religious role of the black church, increasingly criticized its lack of community concern and involvement.[19]

The series focused upon specific contextual issues. In *Children of Bondage* Allison Davis and John Dollard discussed the personality development of black youth in the urban South. Using the case study method the authors attempted to assess "what it means to be born a Negro." They explored the life experiences of "eight selected Negro adolescents" from a wide range of social classes among black as well as white churches and the variations of treatment black youth (and others) received within a fairly well-defined system of caste mores based on socioeconomic status. They discovered from this focused, indepth study that association with and membership in black churches was more the result of a self-selection process on the part of black youth. The youth were more motivated by upward mobility aspirations than the consequence of any exclusionist policy or practice by the churches.

E. Franklin Frazier explored the effects of the migration "from a southern rural to a middle state's urban way of living" upon the personality development of black adolescents. He wanted to know what situations migrating youth faced and what adjustments they had to make given their race, color, and social status. Following a discussion of the black church's role in this transition, Frazier drew four conclusions: 1) the black churches observed generally were not ideologically oriented to assist black youth to esteem their color or status in a white society, despite the fact that God is "good" and "will not suffer discrimination in the other world"; 2) the undue emphasis by black churches on the "other world" caused them to ignore all too often the problems black youth faced; 3) black youth, increasingly affected by the "acids" of secularization surrounding them in the cities, were becoming critical of the black church and "its pretentions as a way of salvation"; 4) youth favored those black churches who seemed to understand them.[20]

In *Growing Up in the Black Belt*, Charles S. Johnson pursues the quest for understanding the personality development of black youth in another context—among rural southern blacks living in an urban Southern community. Johnson understood personality to be the result of the organization of the habits and behavior patterns a person made in adjusting to his or her new environment. Given this basic perspective, Johnson began to develop some understanding of the repulsion rural black youth felt toward city black churches and their programs. The youth found that city church programs did not match their experiences of churches "back home." And in the midst of the many urban society attractions, the youth did not seem to require the church for emotional release as much as their parents did.[21]

The deleterious effects of color discrimination on the personalities of black youth between 1910 and the 1930s was the subject of the research by W. Lloyd Warner, Buford H. Junker, and Walter O. Adams. The results were published in *Color and Human Nature: Negro Personality Development in a Northern City*. Based on case histories of black youth on Chicago's South Side and experiential observation, they developed a three-fold theory regarding the significance of color: 1) white dominance endemic in American society significantly impacts black personality development; 2) negative color evaluations by blacks toward blacks, and 3) the black community's class type, social and occupational status greatly affects black personality formation. Class, status, and color stratification exist in the black church. Moreover black youth, who were skeptical about the church's concern, advocacy and action on color issues broke their ties with the church.[22]

Robert L. Sutherland summarized the American Council of Education Youth Commission's series in *Color, Class, and Personality*. In keeping with the commision's original mandate to study the needs of black youth, appraise facilities, and estimate resources for meeting the problems defined, Sutherland suggested that black youth faced "multiple limitations" and the improvement of their situation must be plural rather than singular. He also concluded that racist thinking about black youth should be eradicated and that fuller recognition should be accorded black youth for the sake of building a stronger nation.[23] The social climate did not provide much encouragement for the realization of these goals through the effort of black churches. Instead writers continued to point to the disparity between the needs of black youth and the church's youth-related programmatic structures. Obviously the nation's legal and social climate did not indicate much enthusiasm for Sutherland's conclusions. In fact, the general lack of interest in improving the needs of black youth may be underscored by the void in further research into black youth experience until the mid-1960s.

However, two articles prior to the Brown and Brown 1954 Supreme Court decision do point to changes in church approaches to black youth. In 1950 Ira L. Gibbons identified that Boy and Girl Scout and YWCA and YMCA programs historically associated with black churches had shifted their emphasis during the previous decade from character-building to youth-serving agencies. He did not explore whether a corresponding change in perspective emerged in church youth programs. In the same year Oscar Lee, while exploring the feelings of black youth toward the church, discovered that urban youth expressed crticism of the church; rural youth were more accepting. Both desired programmatic changes. In a now familiar refrain, Lee concluded that better trained youth leaders were needed in both settings. Both articles pointed to a need in black church youth ministries: the lack of more literature on the subject actually reveals the general lack of attention to the experience of black youth in or out of the church.[24]

Black Youth, Black Church, and the Civil Rights Movement

The civil rights era began with the protest actions for equal treatment under the law in the 1940s. It escalated into the "Freedom Now" movement of the 1950s which

demanded equality of law for all Americans. It witness-
ed the historic Supreme Court decision declaring uncon-
stitutional the infamous concept and practice of "separate but equal" treatment of black youth in public schools
in 1954. It climaxed with the passage of the most comprehensive civil rights legislation in any western nation to
date with 1964 Congressional action defining, affirming,
and guaranteeing equity of access to public accommoda-
tions, education, housing, voting, and employment.

In both the South and North, the black church was
squarely behind the struggle for civil rights. It was in the
South, however, that the struggle was fiercest. If it had
not been for the leadership of men, women, youth, and
students, the majority of whom were members of black
churches, there would not have been a movement. The
incredibly courageous participation of thousands of
people in marches, demonstrations, boycotts, and con-
frontations was a crucial factor in the success of one of
the most effective non-violent protest movements for
human rights in American history. It was a spiritual as
well as a social revolution.

The story of the Christian education among black
youth, however, is not as impressive. During this period
the educational efforts of black churches experienced a
declining vitality. Their combined programs never
reached more than a major fraction of black youth.
Those programs that did exist were conventional, imita-
tive of white models, poorly attended, and were, for the
most part, socially marginal. Historically, black and
white youth programs had developed separately, but
most black youth programs were still indistinguishable
from their white counterparts in educational philosophy,
goals, strategy, program, and leadership style. Perhaps
these factors contributed to a divisive and widening gap

between black churches and their youth by the mid-
sixties. A study of the ghetto's impact on black youth
development puts this conclusion in context. Although
set in Harlem, its discoveries applied to other urban areas
as well.

1. Religion is an important factor in black adolescent
   development, but it is unavailable or inaccessible to the
   majority of black ghetto youth.
2. The important thing religion offers most black youth
   is "a sense of place and purpose in life."
3. The Christian education programs that do exist and
   are accessible to black youth did not perform this
   function well, except perhaps for a relatively small
   number of youth related to the families of church
   members.
4. Generally, black churches in the black communities
   of this period were not significantly involved in the Civil
   Rights movement beyond the participation of individual members and moral support. Actually some felt
   isolated from or ambivalent toward "the struggle."
5. Although black churches at this point (1955-65) were
   committed to the redemption of black youth in the
   ghettoes, creating a sense of place and purpose was not
   reflected intentionally in their educational programs.[25]

   The challenge to the black church embodied in the
Harlem study reflected the more public perspective of
the Black Revolution, which sought to actualize for the
black community the legal enactments it had gained. It
confronted the churches with the inadequacy of its
generally neutral if not conservative social theology and
praxis. It challenged black churches to be pastorally
accountable and responsible to their communities. It
called for a re-evaluation of the preaching, worship,
community outreach, teaching, learning, witness and

service of congregations in ministry in oppressed communities and among generally oppressed peoples.

The need for black churches to establish new directions in their approaches to black youth was clearly recognized by some. Among the first committees appointed by the National Committee of Black Churchmen (NCBC) after its founding in 1967 was an Education Committee (1968). In 1969 members from the black denominations and black representatives of educational staff of predominantly white denominations in the National Council of Churches formed the Black Christian Education Project to address the educational needs of black people, especially those victims of overt oppression. Out of its work emerged the Black Youth Development and Growth project.

This latter program with an emphasis on black youth, formulated an educational design which included components on black history, black church history, Saturday ethnic schools, and role-modeling. The training of leaders, teachers, and workers from across the nation for this project occurred in three major workshops at the Krisheim Study Center in Philadelphia between 1969 and 1971. The third of these conference-workshops dealt with the theme "Black Church and Youth Empowerment." Its purposes reflected the historic concern of black church leaders with strengthening the relationship of black youth to the church. However, these purposes were for the first time, informed by an analysis of the relationship of black youth to the larger youth culture.[26]

Since 1971 the movement toward the indigenization of Christian education has intensified across the black church. In 1971 a group of editors from several black denominations met for the first time to develop black church curriculum resources development. That same

year a Black Ecumenical Curriculum Resources Center
was established by the Joint Education Development department of the National Council of Churches under the
leadership of Joe Nash. In 1973 the Graded Press of The
United Methodist Church released Anthony J. Shipley's
Resources in the Black Church, a practical guide on teaching
and learning with youth in black churches.[27]

Perhaps the most significant, new approach to black
youth ministry is found in the growing number of creative
efforts among some church leaders and congregations to
develop approaches that seriously consider the life situations and experiences of black youth. Romney Moseley
in chapter four describes in detail several of these efforts.
An early example of this increasing innovative energy in
black churches across the country, however, may be seen
in the Educational Growth Organization (EGO) initiated
by Los Angeles AME pastor, John Hurst Adams in 1968.
It has grown from its original sponsoring group of eight
churches into an ecumenical network. The organization
enculturates young people into the black experience,
transmits the African-American heritage, builds self-esteem (all new directions in the church's educational
ministry), and provides for a meaningful Christian education.[28]

Although traditional approaches to black youth ministries continue to prevail and despite the critiques of
scholars and church leaders, the spirit of creativity in
these new approaches indicates that black youth may
increasingly experience a new day in the church. However, it means a more vigorous grasp of their experiences
and a more focused approach to the use of church
resources in their behalf. The next three chapters draw
upon the larger body of research in black theology and
black youth experience to extend that discussion.

──────── *NOTES* ────────

1. W.E.B. DuBois, *The Souls of Black Folk* (Chicago: A.C. McClurg Co., 1903), pp. 189-95.

2. Carter G. Woodson, *The Education of the Negro Prior to 1861* (New York: G.P. Putnam, 1915), Ch. VIII; James D. Tyms, *The Rise of Religious Education Among Negro Baptists* (New York: Exposition Press, 1965), pp. 118-19; Ella P. Mitchell, "Oral Tradition: Legacy of Faith for the Black Church," *Religious Education* 81 (Winter, 1986) # 1, pp. 93-106.

3. Frank O. Erb, *The Development of the Young People's Movement* (Chicago: University of Chicago Press, 1917), pp. 47-53.

4. Charles S. Smith, *History of the African Methodist Episcopal Church* (Philadelphia: Book Concern of the AME Church, 1922), p. 236; William J. Walls, *The African Methodist Episcopal Zion Church* (Charlotte, N.C.: AME Zion Publishing House), p. 289; Tyms, pp. 311-17.

5. Erb, p. 63.

6. Tyms, p. 313; Othal Nathaniel Lakey, *The History of the CME Church* (Memphis: Tenn.: The CME Publishing House, 1985), pp. 306-07.

7. Charles R. Foster, Ethel R. Johnson and Grant S. Shockley, *Christian Education Journey of Black Americans* (Nashville, Tenn.: Discipleship Resources, 1985), p. 14.

8. Cf. E. Franklin Frazier, *The Negro Church in American* (New York: Schocken Books, 1963), pp. 47-49.

9. St. Clair Drake and Horace Cayton, *Black Metropolis: A Study of Negro Life in a Northern City* (New York: Harcourt, Brace, 1945), pp. 520-25.

10. Frazier, p. 50.

11. Carter G. Woodson, *The History of the Negro Church* (Washington, D.C.: The Associated Publishers, 1921 [1945]), pp. 252-60.

12. Frazier, p. 51; Lawrence N. Jones, "The Black Church: A New Agenda" *Where the Spirit Leads: American Denominations Today,* ed., Martin E. Marty (Atlanta: John Knox Press, 1980), p. 49.

13. Garland Penn and J.W.E. Bowen, eds., *The United Negro: His Problems and His Progress* (New York: Negro Universities Press, 1902)., p. XII.

14. W.E.B. DuBois, ed., *The Negro Church* (Atlanta: The Atlanta University Press, 1903), pp. 185-89.

15. W.E.B. DuBois and Augustus G. Dill, eds., *Morals and Manners Among Negro Americans* (Atlanta: The Atlanta University Press, 1914), p. 108; George E. Haynes, "The Negro Church and Our Changing Social Order," *Whither the Negro Church*: Seminar held at Yale (University) Divinity School (New Haven, CT: April 13-15, 1931), p. 20.

16. Benjamin E. Mays and Joseph W. Nicholson, *The Negro Church* (New York: Institute of Social and Religious Studies, 1933), preface.

17. Charles H. Wesley, "The Religious Attitudes of Negro Youth," *Journal of Negro History,* XXI (October 1936) 4, pp.376-93; William E. Carrington, "Negro Youth and the Religious Education Program of the Church," *The Journal of Negro Education,* IX (October 1940) 4, pp.388-96; John Dillingham, *Making Religious Education Effective* (New York: Association Press, 1935), p. 63.

18. F.W. Reeves, "Foreword," in Allison Davis and John Dollard, *Children of Bondage: The Personality Development of Negro Youth in the Urban South* (New York: Harper and Row, 1940), p. V.

19. Ira D. Reid, *In a Minor Key: Negro Youth in Story and Fact* (Washington, D.C.: American Council on Education, 1940), p. 83-87.

20. E. Franklin Frazier, *Negro Youth at the Crossways: Their Personality Development in the Middle States* (New York: Schocken Books, 1940), p. 133.

21. Charles S. Johnson, *Growing Up in the Black Belt: Negro Youth in the Rural South* (Washington, D.C.: American Council on Education, 1941), p. 169.

22. W. Lloyd Warner, Buford H. Junker, and Walter O. Adams, *Color and Human Nature: Negro Personality Development in a Northern City* (Washington, D.C.: American Council on Education, 1941), pp. 6-23, 64-65.

23. Robert L. Sutherland, *Color, Class and Personality* (Washington, D.C.: American Council on Education, 1942), p. 133.

24. Ira L. Gibbons, "Character Building Agencies and the Needs of Negro Children and Youth," *Journal of Negro Education* XIX (Summer 1950) 3, pp.363-71; J. Oscar Lee, "The Religious Life and Needs of Negro Youth," *Journal of Negro Education* XIX (Summer 1950) 3, pp. 298-309.

25. Cf. Lyle E. Schaller, *The Impact of the Future* (Nashville, Tenn.: Abingdon Press, 1969), p. 98; *Youth in the Ghetto: A Study of the Consequence of Powerlessness and a Blueprint for Change* (New York: Harlem Youth Opportunities Unlimited, Inc., 1964), pp. 1, 35, 64-70.

26. Several studies and research articles appeared between 1966-71 relevant to the Krisheim conference emphasis on youth empowerment. Cf. Alvin F. Poussaint, "The Negro American: His Self-Image and Integration"

which documents the general presence of identity and self-image problems in black children, youth and adults which he suggests must be resolved "through political and social group action, racial solidarity, [and] programs of black consciousness." Presented at the 71st meeting of the National Medical Association, Chicago (August 8, 1966), p. 7; In "Search for Identity" Kenneth B. Clark discussed the street riots involving black youth in the sixties as the manifestation of the quest for self-esteem...the unavoidable symptom(s) of...positive transition and (a) sign of health...;" *Ebony Magazine* (August 1967); Bishop Caesar D. Coleman of the CME Church in "Agenda for the Black Church," recognized that "this generation of young black Americans are some of the best equipped youth in the world for effective constructive social change [and] the black church must lead youth beyond blackness to destiny," *Religious Education* (November-December 1969), p. 445; On the other side of this optimism, Paul Nichols in his unpublished dissertation, concluded that curriculum materials enhancing black self-esteem, whether from black or white publishing sources, were minimal; "The Extent to Which Curriculum Materials Reflect the Black Experience," (Washington, D.C.: The American University, 1976). C. Eric Lincoln has cautioned church leaders that "black youth do not rule out summarily the legitimacy of some other religion for black people, but it must be a religion untainted by white association or white manipulation"; "White Christianity and Black Commitment: A Comment on the Power of Faith and Socialization," *The Journal of the Interdenominational Theological Center*, VI (Fall 1978), p. 22.

27.   Anthony J. Shipley, *Resources in the Black Church* (Nashville, Tenn.: The Graded Press, 1973).

28.   John Hurst Adams, "Saturday Ethnic School," *Spectrum* (July-August 1971) pp. 8-9, 32.

CHAPTER TWO

Psychosocial Experiences

JANICE HALE-BENSON

Editor's introduction: After family, school undoubtedly effects the experience of African-American youth more than other influence. Many writers have explored this ambiguity: Most emphasize the importance of schooling in the preparation of young people for adult roles and responsibilities. Some point to the school's dominance of traditional European-American values and procedures.

In the following essay, Dr. Janice Hale-Benson explores learning styles of black children for the experience of African American youth in and through the church. Her work is controversial because it begins with the premise that there is an African American cultural way of learning and creating meaning from life experiences. She claims that for African American children and youth this distinctive learning style is disregarded for the most part in the school experience. She insists, however, that it must be taken seriously in black youth ministries if they are to develop the skills to negotiate their way in the church and larger society. Additionally, the learning style must foster a strong sense of self-esteem and a clear view of the contributions they might make to others.

JUST BECAUSE

Just because I don't sing
Doesn't mean I ain't a singer.

Doesn't mean I ain't a star.
Just because you don't see me
Doesn't mean I ain't there.

I am here
Growing quietly
Growing strong
Day by day
Striving on
Past my youth
Past my play
Looking on
Looking ahead
Waiting my turn.[1]

*I*n considering the church's ministry to black youth, it is critical to acknowledge the structural oppression of African Americans in this society. We cannot effectively analyze the parts without a consideration of the whole. Likewise, we must only consider solutions in the context of the total African American liberation struggle.

Tillman and Tillman, in *Why American Needs Racism and Poverty*, have concluded that black people, wherever they are found in the world, are in a colonial relationship with white people. This colonial system has perpetuated their political, economic, and cultural exploitation. Regardless of where it is found—America, Africa, the Caribbean—the system achieves the same end: exploiting the labor power and resources of the colonized.

The Tillmans suggest further that the original form of this exploitation in America was slavery; but when slavery ended, it was replaced by other systems that recreated the relationship of one group at the bottom to the other group at the top. These subsequent mechanisms for oppressing people in a system of colonialism have included slavery, sharecropping, disenfranchisement, political control, forced labor, racism, dual labor and housing markets, and systematic cultural repression. These mechanisms seldom function alone but as parts of a coherent whole. They form a system maintaining the domination of the white group and the oppression of the black group.

Important in the working of this system is a dual labor and housing market linked to the educational system. Each of these institutions forms an interlocking web so that political and economic domination gives rise to cultural domination, which in turn reinforces political and economic domination. Inferior education in ghetto schools handicaps black workers in the labor market. Blacks are then discriminated against in employment, and this creates low wages and frequent unemployment. With low incomes, blacks have difficulty obtaining good housing. Lack of good education, low-level occupations, and exclusion from ownership and control of large enterprises prevent blacks from developing political power: thus they cannot change basic housing, planning, educational programs. The limitations reinforce the total oppression of black people.

The consequences for black children and youth are significant. The masses are disproportionately located in families suffering from the turmoil of unemployment, single parent heads of households, and low-paying occupational positions. This causes them to be at high risk for family instability and deprivation. Bruce Hare makes that clear in these circumstances:

> ...they are also more likely to fall victim to child abuse, inadequate nutrition, poor health care, drugs, crime,

and material deprivation. They are more likely to live in below-par, crowded quarters, with relatives other than their biological parents, and in foster care. Given such possibilities as these, it is a wonder that they survive and thrive as well as they do. Fortunately, indicators are that they are loved and feel loved, but there is no denying that many Black youth must also suffer the consequences of the pressures under which they and their parents live.[2]

Hare goes on to blame the endangered status of black youth on the structural inequality of the American educational and occupational systems. "The myth of equal opportunity," he suggests, "serves as a smoke screen through which the losers will be led to blame themselves, and be seen by others as getting what they deserve."[3] The educational system, through its unequal skill giving, grading, routing and credentialing procedures plays a critical role in fostering structured inequality in the American social system. The occupational structure simply responds to the schools when it slots people into hierarchical positions based on credentials and skills given by the schools.

The dire statistics on the compendium of problems of black youths are well known. How do black children endowed with innate equal childhood potential arrive at such a disadvantaged youth status? That question explores what in the schools reproduces failure in black children generation after generation. Schools do function as the major socializing institution in our society. Students who drop out, are pushed out, or are provided a diminished education are disconnected from a viable future. Other problems confronting black youth such as teen pregnancy, crime, drugs, and unemployment emanate from school failure.

It is our thesis that black children do not enter school disadvantaged. They emerge from school as disadvantaged youth. For this reason the church *must* evaluate its ministries to black youth based in part on an accurate assessment of the core causes of the challenges they face. It necessitates confronting the difficulties children and youth experience in negotiating the school.

Black Youth and the Loss of a Viable Future

One explanation for the difficulties black children experience in school may be traced to their birth into a culture that is very different from the culture which designed the school. In *Black Children*,[4] I argue for examining the cultural core for black children in general while acknowledging that lower income children are most severely affected by the dual socialization required to straddle Afro- and Euro-American cultures. I would like to go a step further and consider scholarship, which examines the specific interethnic code conflict that transpires between black children and white teachers and results in failure over time for black children, as they move into adolescence.

Ray McDermott offers an interesting starting point for our analysis when he calls black Americans a pariah group in American society. Frederick Barth defines a pariah group as any group "actively rejected by the host population because of behavior or characteristics positively condemned" by dominant group standards.[5] McDermott observes that in a pariah group each generation of children renews the lifestyle of their parents, oblivious to the oppression that the host group brings. This insight challenges the view that the host population works actively to defeat the efforts of each and every pariah child to overcome the cycle of degradation that is his or her birthright. Racial markers, low prestige dialects, school failure, occupational specialties, and lifestyles tag each new generation for low-ascribed status.

McDermott poses the alternative thesis that *failure* is also an *achievement*.[6] He points out that inherited disadvantage as simple tagging is a simplistic explanation. Overt negative ascriptions are frowned upon in popular ideologies, and have been limited by legislation. Yet the pariah boundaries remain firm throughout the society and in school systems. Even without formal institutionalized ascription, pariah status survives into each successive generation. He suggests that:

> The host population does not simply slot a child on the basis of its parentage and then keep a careful eye out for the child so that he (sic) never advances a slot. Rather, it seems as if the child must learn how to do it himself; he must learn a way of acting normally which the host population will be able to condemn according to the criteria the hosts have learned for evaluating, albeit arbitrarily, their own normal behavior. Pariah status appears almost as achieved as ascribed.[7]

Each new pariah generation affirms the soundness of this classificatory system because it learns and exemplifies the behavior essential to the system's maintenance. Rather than regarding themselves blinded by prejudice, the hosts maintain that they are using evaluation standards that are uniform for all people regardless of race or ethnic identity. McDermott wonders, however, how they know "that what is there for them to see is in fact there?"[8]

He observes that pariah groups do not enter school disadvantaged; they leave school disadvantaged. Ascription of status does not account for all of this disadvantage;

nor do the inherent characteristics of the pariah population account for the disadvantage. Clearly the pariah
group regards the host behavior as oppressive. Likewise,
the host group regards the pariah behaviors as inadequate. McDermott suggests that how the two groups learn
this about each other is the central problem.

Misunderstanding often take place in the early grades
and the results are disastrous. When "a host teacher treats
a child as inadequate," the child finds "the teacher oppressive." Upon finding a teacher oppressive, the child
often starts behaving in ways the teacher finds inadequate. Inevitably the relationship between the child and
the teacher regresses—"the objectionable behavior of
each will feed back negatively into the objectionable
behavior of the other."[9]

McDermott maintains that a child must *achieve* pariah
status. This status is neither totally ascribed nor naturally
acquired by the child. Interethnic code differences cause
miscommunication between the teacher and the child.
As their communication continues to deteriorate the
children eventually form alternatives to the teacher's
organization of the classroom. They construct this new
social organization in an attempt to become visible. This
results in more condemnation of their behavior and the
teacher becomes the administrator *in charge of failure.*

"Teachers do not simply ascribe minority children to
failure. Nor do minority children simply drag failure
along, either genetically or socially, from the previous
generation." Instead the status of achieved failure "must
be worked out in every classroom, every day, by every
teacher and every child in their own peculiar ways.[10] In
McDermott's view, school failure becomes an achievement because it is a rational adaptation made by children
to human relations in host schools. Children produce

pariah-host statuses in their interactions with each other and their teachers.

Young children are vulnerable to messages of relationship. McDermott explains that this sensitivity can have direct consequences for their success in school.

> School success, an essential ingredient in any child's avoidance of pariah status, is dependent upon high levels of information transfer. In these early stages of school, depending upon how the politics of every day life are handled, the child defines his (sic) relations with his classmates and his teachers. These relations, remember, define the context of whatever information is to be transferred by a communicant. If the wrong messages of relationship are communicated, reading, writing, and arithmetic may take on very different meanings than they do for the child who is more successful in getting good feelings from the politics of the classroom. The wrong messages can result in learning disabilities.[11]

Erik Erikson makes a similar point in his discussion of the formative experiences during puberty: "it is of great relevance" to the identity formation of young people that they be responded to and given function and status as persons "whose gradual transformation makes sense to those who begin to makes sense"[12] to them.

The teacher plays an important role in organizing the statuses and identities of children in the classroom. One example of the social organization of status and identity in the classroom according to McDermott occurs through the division of the class into ability groups. This division is made to simplify classroom administration. It also determines the level of work engaged in, the people to be interacted with, and the kind of feedback received from the teacher. He notes that children rarely reject the assignment they receive—even to the lowest status groups. Instead they accept their assignment as if it makes sense. A child who rejects this status designation often works hard to catch up with the rest of the class in an effort to prove the designation wrong.

The reason revolt is rarely attempted, McDermott suggests is that generally teachers assign host children to groups using criteria that the children use in dealing with each other, or criteria that their parents and the rest of the community use in relating to them. Essentially, the teacher, the children, and the child's community are in agreement. Even if a child is placed in a low-status group, it does not have a disastrous effect if it makes sense. "The politics of everyday life...outside the classroom and the children's world will be in order."[13]

The social organization of ethnic children by a dominant or host group teacher does not proceed as smoothly. There is a reduced possibility that such a teacher will organize the classroom into the same ability groups that the ethnic community might perceive. If the wrong children are assigned to the lower ability group, they will reject the messages of relationship from the teacher. They will demand a political reorganization of the classroom and a relationship that is more in keeping with their self-concepts.

If the teacher is insensitive to their demands, no matter how subtle, then for the remainder of the year the teacher and the children will be engaged in small battles over the status and identities of the children. The resolution of these battles will determine whether anything gets done in the classroom. Thus we can see how the politics of daily classroom life may determine both the amount of information transfer and the development of individual abilities and disabilities.

The development of abilities and disabilities is based significantly on our human tendency to attend to, think about, and manipulate selected aspects of our environments. The "parts of an environment" that "are attended and mastered" depends upon how "the social meaning of the environment" is "recorded in the experiences of the developing child." Attention to reading materials, for example, will depend upon "whether looking in a book is an acceptable activity in a particular social milieu and whether books contain information helpful to operating in a particular social environment."[14]

A chronic educational problem is located in the high rate of learning disabilities found among black children. Numerous explanations for this disproportionality generally suggest some genetic inferiority or cultural deprivation. McDermott suggests, in contrast, that it is caused by selective inattention developed in the politics of everyday life in the classroom. The social work between white teachers and black children over the tasks of status and identity is such a failure that the children turn off and physiologically shut down. The children disattend reading materials and choose to join their peers in the pupil subculture within the class culminating in reading disabilities and school failure for a disproportionate number. Deprivation theorists generally place the fault on the child or the child's culture. However, achieved failure theorists suggest that their measurements of achievement have used a biased set of standards. McDermott asserts that achievements take place in social context. Instead of looking at the skills stored in children's bodies, we must look at the social contexts in which the skills are turned into achievements.

Scores on perception, intelligence, attitude, language, and even neurological tests are remnants of the practical work of persons in a specific situation. Test scores have discernible roots in the social world, although they do not reveal much about the social processes in which a subject is engaged. Cazden, for example, has described black children who do badly on language tests in formal situations and very well in informal situations; the opposite pattern is true for white children.

McDermott points out that tests reveal a great deal about the thinking underlying the social acts to be performed during the test. Reading is an act which may align black children with incompatible forces in their social universe. In the classroom social organization, produced by the politics of everyday life, reading takes its place as part of the teacher's "ecology of games."[15] To read is to buy into the teacher games and all of the statuses and identities that accompany them. Not to read is to buy into the peer group games and the accompanying statuses and identities. In some sense, reading failure becomes a *social accomplishment* that is supported and rewarded by the peer group.

This phenomenon is not measured by tests. The battle lines that determine whether a child learns to read or not are drawn by the statuses and identities made available by the teacher and the peer group. McDermott concludes that when "the teacher and the children can play the same games, then reading and all other school materials will be easily absorbed."[16] However, when the classroom is divided into two separate worlds, with teachers and children playing different games, the classroom organization is altered and the teacher's authority and patterns of information transfer are challenged.

An issue related to reading instruction is located in the struggle for attention. Phillip W. Jackson found in a study of gaze direction, that more than 90 percent of host children had their eyes fixed on the teacher or reading material at a given time. In Harlem elementary schools, the teachers spent more than half their day calling children to attention. Attention patterns seem to be the crux of the struggle in pariah education.[17] In pariah classrooms, there are teacher games and peer group games. The side one chooses will determine to whom one pays attention. To attend to the teacher is to give the teacher a leadership role; to attend to the peer group is to challenge the teacher's authority. McDermott concludes that "those who attend learn to read; those who do not attend do not learn to read."[18]

To Summarize the Discussion of Achieved Failure

Pariah children in host classrooms learn in subtle ways to behave in new, culturally appropriate ways which will cause them to acquire pariah status. The process of learning to behave in a culturally appropriate way in a black classroom that is administered by a white teacher involves learning to disattend teacher and school-produced cues, such as demands for attention or the introduction of new tasks such as reading.

McDermott suggests that these attention patterns are deeply programmed in the central nervous system. When children attempt to attend to cues outside of their normal perceptual patterns, they fail. In this way, when many black children fail in reading, it appears to be the result of a neurological impairment. The children are not actually impaired at all. They have merely learned over time to attend to different stimuli in a school situation. However, this phenomenon results in their being categorized as disabled and treated as inferior.

Communicative Code Differences

George Spindler has demonstrated that middle-class teachers attend middle-class children and label them the most talented and ambitious children in the class. School success follows parallel patterns. Lower class children over time give up trying and amass failing "institutional biographies" as they move through school because they are unable to give evidence of their intelligence in terms of the limited code that teachers use for evaluating children.[19]

Black children are particularly at risk for being overlooked because of a non-recognition of Afro-American culture or its contribution to the school culture. I have pointed out elsewhere that western social science overly emphasizes linguistic and logicomathematical skills in assessing intelligence. Even these skills must be demonstrated in patterns that approximate those used by Anglo-Americans to be recognized by the educational system. In contrast, skills that emerge from black culture are only recognized when they are extraordinary and marketable to the capitalist ecosystem, such as the athletic skills of Michael Jordon or the musical skills of Michael Jackson. When these skills are exhibited in early childhood as a part of a pattern that, if nurtured, could support the self-esteem and achievement of black children, they are virtually ignored.

Ray C. Rist analyzes the effect of dividing a kindergarten classroom into three "ability groups," the fast, slow, and nonlearners at Tables 1, 2 and 3, respectively:

> The organization of the kindergarten classroom according to the expectation of success or failure after the *eighth day of school* (emphasis mine) became the basis for

the differential treatment of the children for the remainder of the school year. From the day that the class was assigned permanent seats, the activities in the classroom were perceivably different from previously. The fundamental division of the class into those expected to learn and those expected not to permeated the teacher's orientation to the class.[20]

The teacher's subjective evaluations were shown by Rist to be rooted in the teacher's evaluation of the children's physical appearance and interactional and verbal behavior. At Table 1 were children with neater and cleaner clothes, lighter skin and a higher attendance pattern on cold days. Class leaders and direction givers were also clustered at Table 1. The children sitting at the low tables spoke less in class, used heavy dialect and seldom spoke to the teacher.

By the time the children were in the third grade, the ones who started out at the lower tables were still at the lower tables. Once a child is tracked, it is difficult to break loose from that designation. The lower the table, the less instructional time the child receives. This child is well on the way to amassing an institutional biography that will follow him or her year by year through the school. This sorting process continues until each year more and more are sorted out until a select few reach college. McDermott states that the "select few make it to college on the basis that they are most like their teachers."[21]

The children at Table 3 are not neurologically impaired slow learners. There is nothing wrong with their native ability. They will just be directing their achievement efforts away from the school. The reason these children were not selected for achievement in their early years relates to the communicative code conflict between them and their teachers. If they are not able to work out this code conflict in the early years, the children at the lower tables take flight into their own subculture which becomes oppositional to the classroom culture constructed by the teacher.

A key to the construction of this alternative classroom culture is the fact that children are assigned to the lower groups together. The larger numbers can construct a more powerful revolt. A normal developmental shift occurs away from the teacher and toward the peer group in fourth, fifth and sixth grade. Therefore, the achievement gap between black and white children becomes most apparent in late elementary school.

The children in the host classroom have three choices. They can take the school as a source of identity as do the children at Table 1. Or, they can take the peer group as a source of identity as do the children at Tables 2 and 3. Many of these children are transformed into gangs by late elementary school. The third and worst choice is represented by the children at the lower tables who accept the teacher's definitions of them and their abilities and passively fail through school into pariah status.

These children not only fail in school, they fail in their identity work. Children are better off who dispute the messages of relationship sent by the teacher and cause disruption in the classroom because they have a better chance of constructing a solid ego in their community that could lead to achievement by an alternative route. The children who passively accept subordinate status do not disrupt the calm classroom status quo, but emerge from the educational experience with a weak ego. McDermott observes that in either response, "learning is blocked; in the first case by active selective inattention and misbehavior, in the second case with motivational lag and selective inattention. Neither group learns to read."[22]

McDermott points out that host group teachers do not create this code difference. Both the children and the teachers participate in the ethnic group traditions they bring to school. In the early years teachers make the difference because they are not as adaptable as the children. However, in later years as the peer group gains strength, the children force the distinction between their code and the teacher's code. In *making their code a difference*, they are learning how to produce pariah status for themselves vis-a-vis the host group.

Ethnic Group Identity and Mobility

Why do blacks not fare as well as other ethnic groups in working out the politics of the classroom? A possible explanation is found in the work of Robert Havighurst who suggests a compatibility between the white Anglo-Saxon, Protestant, and middle-class mainstream and the ethnic cultures of European whites, Jews, Chinese and Japanese.[23] Blacks and Hispanics must shed more of the beliefs, values, attitudes and behavioral styles associated with their ethnicity in order to acquire the somewhat divergent culture of the middle-class mainstream that dominates the school. A dual socialization or straddling of the two cultures is consequently required for upward mobility. His work reinforces my own view that at the root of the achievement and disciplinary difficulties of black children in the large American society is a lack of understanding of an Afro-American oriented culture of the school.

The research of Donald Henderson and Alfonzo Washington into Afro-American cultural patterns may have implications for educational practice. They first affirm that black children are culturally different from white children. This difference can be directly attributed to the fact that black children mature in communities that are culturally different from the communities of the broader society.

> The experience through which the Black child develops his (sic) sense of self, his social orientation, and his world view are provided by institutions (such as family, religion) whose characters, structures and functions are very often unique to the Black community. The school, on the other hand, reflects the culture of the wider society and is often unaccommodative to the culturally different Black youngsters.
> Indeed, often these differences are defined as deficiencies. These deficiencies are assumed to be significant impediments to "proper" learning in school. Therefore, massive attempts at remediation are undertaken (often, to the detriment of the child). In effect, many school practices are inappropriate for treating the educational needs of Black youngsters. An appropriate treatment of the educational needs of Black youngsters must take into account their unique cultural attributes.[24]

I have made the point in *Black Children*, that Afro-American males participate in a culture distinguished from that of Euro-American males and females and Afro-American females. Nonrecognition of this culture, in my opinion, accounts for the disproportionate assignment of black males to low-ability tracts and disciplinary measures while in school.

Christine Bennett and J. John Harris studied the disproportionality of suspensions and expulsions of male and black students. Their findings reveal some surprising characteristics of disrupting students. Serious disrupters, for example, come to school with a strikingly high sense of personal efficacy. They report positive feelings about school. When they get into trouble, they tend to feel that their punishment has been reasonable and fair. The researchers suggest that even though the disruptive students have a sense of overall personal efficacy, they lack a sense of personal efficacy *concerning the school.* They suggest further that this contrast in feeling between *personal* and school efficacy may help explain the disproportionate numbers of males who are suspended and expelled from schools.[25]

It is also evident that black males suffer because of a preference for the behavioral styles of females in educational settings. Catherine Cornbleth and Willard Korth, for example, suggest that in addition to the Euro-American cultural orientation of the school, the teachers in their study reported that white females had a higher potential as learners than white males, black females and black males, in that order.[26] They linked the characteristics of white females (reserved, efficient, orderly, quiet) with learning potential. They also designated the characteristics of black males (outspoken, aggressive, outgoing) as being linked with low potential as learners.

Bruce Hare notes that as early as preadolescence, black children show a trend toward higher peer self-esteem than white children and higher ratings of the importance of being popular and good at sports. His research substantiates that of Bennett and Harris in noting that black children do not differ from white children in general self-esteem or in home self-esteem, but tend toward lower *school self-esteem.* This is accompanied by significantly lower standardized reading and mathematics performance. There seems to be a shift from school to peers that solidifies by late elementary school as pointed out above by McDermott. Given the vulnerability and family turmoil of lower income black youth in particular, this shift toward the positive strokes and affective support of the peer group is a flight from the failure and ego damage of the school.

Hare defines black youth culture as a *long-term failure arena.* On a short-term basis, black youths exhibit competent, adaptive behavior and achieve in the arenas that are open to them. They demonstrate street-wiseness. They excel in playground sports, sexuality, domestic and child-rearing chores. They supplement family income and take on other adult roles at an early age.

Even though this youth culture provides alternative outlets for achievement, it offers little hope for long-term legitimate success. Instead, it carries for youth the danger of being drafted into the self-destructive worlds of drugs, crime and sexual promiscuity. Hare observes that the collectively negative schooling experiences of black youth produces this anti-school sentiment. The accompanying availability of positive peer group experiences and the youth's inability to perceive the long-term consequences of adolescent decisions causes them to make what appears to be a logical decision to shift their attention from the school to the peers.

Implications for the Church and
Its Efforts to Connect Black Youth to the Future

A primary goal of the church's ministry to black youth must be to connect them to a viable future. This can only be done after an incisive analysis of the problems they face and an identification of the quicksand and landmines they confront as they move from early childhood through adolescence.

Unfortunately, the black community does not control the schools which set the stage for failure throughout the life span. However, through accurate analysis of the shortfall of the schools, the church can stand, as it has throughout the black experience in America, in a continuing supportive role to the children and youth.

One obvious role that the black church has served and must continue to serve is in the area of self-concept development, leadership development and the projection of positive role models for black children and youth. With the attacks on the self-images and self-esteem of black youth that have been described above, the church must continue to serve as an arena forachievement in developing speaking skills, skills in the expressive arts and co-curricular activities that enrich academic achievement. More specific implications include the following:

1. *The church must remove critical barriers to achievement for Afro-American children and youth.* For example, the control of fertility is a critical issue in Afro-American female adolescent development. The majority of babies in the black community born are to 12- to 20-year-old females. Black professional couples, in contrast, are not even reproducing themselves.

Apparently, black middle-class women have learned that low fertility is key to a middle-class lifestyle because they have a significantly lower birthrate than white middle-class women. Given the fact black women have the lowest income of any group in the society and the fact that 48% of black families are headed by women, a low fertility rate makes sense for those who desire some semblance of a middle-class lifestyle. There is a major communication breakdown in transmitting this reality to lower income black women. Fortunately, some communities have cre-

ated commendable programs in which a big sister relationship is created between professional black women to
provide role models and direct guidance to girls in the
community whose futures are at risk for having babies at
such young ages.

Another important issue for the church to address is
how to increase the numbers of black males who com-
plete high school, as well as enroll and graduate from
college. Black males receive very little information about
how to bridge their youth peer culture and amass long
term achievements. Robert Staples has identified the
college educated black male as one who has learned how
to develop long-term achievements. Ninety percent of
college-educated black males are married and living with
their spouses. Even though they earn less on the average
than a white high school drop out, they still live longer and
have a higher quality of life than their less well educated
counterparts.

A promising approach to ministries with black adolescent males complements cultural values and attitudes
already present in Afro-American culture. Strengthening
the bond between achievement in sports which are
emphasized in black culture and academic achievement
is illustrative. Attention should be given to the role of
coaches who like John Thompson of George-town University produce winning teams and black male graduates,
and to the effective use of athletic scholarships in strengthening black male achievement.

2. *The church can also give attention to and place pressure
upon schools to improve the educational outcomes of black
children and youth.* Connecting black youth to the future
involves monitoring the curriculum of schools to ensure
that it is preparing them to acquire the technological
skills necessary for employment in the 1990s. A National

Urban Coalition study reveals the problem facing black children and youth. Although 80% of the jobs offered to college graduates in the 1990s will be in the engineering sciences, only 11% of black seniors in 1980 and 1982 had taken the advanced mathematics required for those majors. In contrast 60% of the Asian American and 30% of the white seniors had taken trigonometry, calculus, and other advanced math courses. In that same 1980 and 1982 study, 27% of the Asian American and 13% of the white seniors took Physics I. Only 5.5% of black high school seniors took first year physics.

These figures contrast with a National Assessment of Educational Progress report (1982) which included items designed to assess *student attitudes* towards science. Forty-seven percent of the 13-year-old white students indicated positive attitudes toward science. This study revealed that 50% of the 13-year-old black students indicated positive attitudes toward science. Further, the National Urban Coalition indicated that 15% of third grade black students expressed an interest in technical occupations. What happens to that interest?

Study should be made to explore why these positive attitudes and interests are not translating into achievement in these arenas. The National Urban Coalition states that black children do not see people who look like them doing math and science in textbooks. Perhaps an overemphasis occurs on figures in the civil rights struggle in the creation of heroes in the black community. Visible role models in technological careers are needed for black children and youth. The churches can heighten the sensitivity of school officials at this point.

3. *Finally, the church can continue to make a contribution to strengthening family life in the black community.* In his recent study of the relationship between family life and school

achievement, Reginald Clark dispels myths about the limitations of family structure or income on children's school achievement.[27] He discovered that school problems had more to do with the character of family culture than the presence of working mothers, broken homes, poverty, racial or ethnic background, or poorly educated parents.

Clark based his conclusions on intimate case studies of ten black families in Chicago. All of the families had income at the poverty level and were equally divided between one-parent and two-parent families. All were likewise equally divided in terms of having produced either a high- or low-achieving child. Clark made detailed observations on the quality of home life, noting how family habits and interactions affected school achievement and what characteristics of family life provided children with "school survival skills." His work suggests that the church can assist black parents in learning to inculcate school survival skills in their children.

This chapter is designed to convey something of the complicated process that consistently holds black Americans at the bottom of the educational and occupational ladder. A central argument is that churches need to engage in the incisive analysis of the problems of black children and youth in the schools so that we can focus our efforts and dwindling resources on the agonizingly slow process of trying to effect meaningful change for a generation of black youths. To do less is to risk losing an entire generation.

———— *NOTES* ————

1. Ja J. Jahannes, "Just Because," National Black Child Development Institute Calender, 1987.

2. Bruce Hare, "Structural Inequality and the Endangered Status of Black Youth," *Journal of Negro Education*, 56 (Winter 1987) #1, p. 104.

3. *Ibid.*, p. 101.

4. Janice Hale-Benson, *Black Children: Their Roots, Culture and Learning Styles* (Baltimore John Hopkins University Press, 1986). I locate myself clearly among the theorists who trace the genesis of black culture to its African heritage, while acknowledging that there are other theories. The discussion over these theories is lively because the evidence supporting each is still inconclusive.

5. Quoted by Ray McDermott, "Achieving School Failure: An Anthropological Approach to Literary and Social Stratification," in *Education and Cultural Process: Anthropological Approches*, ed., George D. Spindler, (Prospect Heights, Ill., Waveland Press, 1987), p.174.

6. *Ibid.*, p. 176.

7. *Ibid.*

8. *Ibid.*, p. 178.

9. *Ibid.*

10. *Ibid.*

11. *Ibid.*, p. 181.

12. Erik Erikson, *Identity: Youth and Crisis* (New York: Norton, 1968), p. 156.

13. McDermott, p. 183.

14. *Ibid.*, p. 184.

15. Courtney B. Cazden, "The Situation: A Neglected Source of Social Class Differences in Language Use," *Journal of Social Issues*, 26 (Spring 1971) #2, pp. 35-60; Norton E. Long. "The Local Community as an Ecology of Games," *Politics of Social Life*, eds., Nelson Polsby, et. al. (Boston: Houghton Mifflin Company, 1958) p. 408.

16. McDermott, p. 186. Several other researchers have similarly noted the success of educational settings directed by teachers of children of the same ethnic and dialect minorities in contrast to the failure of educational settings directed by outsiders. Cf. Susan Biele Alitto, "The Language Issue in Communist Chinese Education," in *Aspects of Chinese Education*, ed. C. T. Hu (New York: Teachers College Press, 1968), pp. 43-59; John A. Hostetler and Gertrude E. Huntington, *Children in Amish Society: Socialization and Community Education* (New York: Holt, Rinehart,

and Winston, Inc., 1971); Joshua A. Fishman and Erika Leuders-Salmon, "What Has Sociology to Say to the Teachers," in *Functions of Speech in the Classroom*, eds., Courtney B. Cazden, et. al. (New York: Teachers College Press, 1972), pp. 67-83.

17. Cf. Phillip Wesley Jackson, *Life in the Classroom* (New York: Holt, Rinehart, and Winston, Inc., 1968); Martin Deutsch, "The Disadvantaged Child and the Learning Process," in *Education in Depressed Areas*, ed., A. Harry Passow (New York: Teacher College Press, 1963); Joan I. Roberts, *Scene of the Battle: Group Behavior in Urban Classrooms* (New York: Doubleday Company, 1970).

18. McDermott, p. 190.

19. Cf. George D. Spindler, ed., "The Transmission of American Culture," in *Education and Culture*, (New York: Holt, Rinehart, and Winston, Inc., 1963); Erving Goffman, *Stigma* (Englewood Cliffs, N.J.: Prentice Hall, Inc. 1963).

20. Ray C. Rist, "Student Social Class and Teacher Expectations," *Harvard Educational Review*, 40 (August 1970) #3, p. 423.

21. McDermott, p. 198.

22. *Ibid.*, p. 199.

23. Robert J. Havighurst, "The Relative Importance of Social Class and Ethnicity in Human Development," *Human Development*, 19 (1976) #1, pp. 56-64.

24. Donald H. Henderson and Alfonzo G. Washington, "Cultural Differences and the Education of Black Children: An Alternative Model for Program Development," *Journal of Negro Education*, 44 (1975), p. 353.

25. Christine Bennett and J. John Harris, III, "Suspensions and Expulsions of Male and Black Students: A Study of the Causes of Disproportionality," *Urban Education*, 16 (1982) #4, p. 419.

26. Catherine Cornbleth and Willard Korth, "Teacher Perceptives and Teacher-Student Interaction in Integrated Classrooms," *Journal of Experimental Education*, 48 (Summer 1963), pp. 259-63.

27. Reginald M. Clark, *Family Life and School Achievement: Why Poor Black Children Succeed or Fail* (Chicago: The University of Chicago Press, 1983), pp. 1-3, 197-201.

CHAPTER THREE

A Theological Framework

JACQUELYN GRANT

Editor's introduction: In the following essay Jacqueline Grant begins with the assumption that black theology is the impetus in youth ministry. Youth ministry purposes and strategies drawn from traditional European American theologies miss the mark. Consequently Dr. Grant proposes a theological framework that might more appropriately guide the development of programmatic and curricular structures for black youth ministry.

When I entered seminary I brought with me two things: a call to leadership based on my involvement in leadership roles in the church from an early age, and a call to Christian education heightened by my awareness, through the civil rights/black power movement of the sixties, of the cry of black church people for relevancy in Christian education. I had searched for church school curriculum revelant to the black religious experience, but could not find it. Later this call to Christian education was expanded to the call to ordained ministry.

I hoped a degree in Christian education would help me create what I called relevant educational resources for the black church. After entering seminary, however, I quickly discovered that the question of relevancy extended far beyond the Christian education department. I discovered Christian education resources can only be adequate when the theology which serves as their foundation is adequate. Bad theology produces bad Christian education resources; irrelevant theology produces irrelevant resources; oppressive theology produces oppressive resources. With this realization, I shifted disciplines from Christian education to my fourth calling and final field of study, theology.

Christian education (indeed all forms of ministry) has theological foundations. Ministry—its character, relevance, quality, and value—is determined by its theological foundation. This chapter explores various dimensions of theology vis-a-vis the church's ministry to black youth. The first focus is upon the doctrine of humanity. Theology is a secondary act which begins with human beings. This exploration cover four points: 1) The Task of Theology; 2) Experience, Empowerment, and Theology; 3) On Becoming Human—Somebodiness of the Black Person; 4) Implications for the Black Church and its Ministry to Black Youth.

The Task of Theology

Theology as an area of inquiry has involved two significant parties—people and God. It involves our human interpretations of God and the Christian faith in our historical and contemporary settings. Owen Thomas suggests that our efforts to write theology encompasses a three-fold task. 1) Theology determines the essentials of the Christian faith. 2) Theology teaches and explains the meaning and requirement of the Christian faith. 3) Theology translates the thought world of the Bible for us today— differentiating a first century world view from our contemporary world view.[1]

For centuries, however, this three-fold task has been carried out by white males. Careful examination reveals that male theologians have offered interpretations more than sympathetic to their own dominant culture. The essentials of Christian faith have been confused with the essentials of being a member of the dominant culture. Moreover, in much theological writing, being Christian has been confused with being white. Theology, though handed down to us as pure and universal, has actually been a particular theology.

This "white theology"—as it has been called—has undergirded ideologies of white supremacy ensuring the beliefs in the superiority of whites and the inferiority of nonwhites. For too long, this superiority/inferiority understanding has served as the basis for domination and submission relationships between the races in the institutions of our society.

The development of black theology as a discipline challenged systematically this way of thinking. Black scholars have demonstrated a vital connection between exclusivistic, oppressive, ivory tower theologies and the victimized status of black people. In their rereading of scripture they discovered that God worked consistently on the side of the victimized—the oppressed of society. This rereading led the foremost black theologian, James Cone, to speak of "a theology of liberation." As the rational study of the being God in the world in light of the existential situation of an oppressed community, it relates the forces of liberation to the essence of the gospel, which is Jesus Christ.[2]

Theology from this perspective is directly related to the praxis of liberation; that is, theology arises out of the experience of people, reflecting and discerning God's activity in the midst of their own liberation. As a liberation praxis oriented theology, doctrinal revisions become paramount if we are to understand the true task of theology. The question for us is, how do we reconstruct theological doctrines in order to reflect the liberating focus of the gospel?

God as the chief agent of liberation is a critical affirmation, but what is of equal importance is the doctrine of humanity. The "who are we?" question has bearing upon who we say God is. The doctrine of humanity then is of utmost importance for comprehending the meaning of God, because human beings are responsible for theological concepts. These concepts, based upon our interpretations of the gospel, reflect the lived experiences of people. Historically, that experience has been an oppressive one for black people, women, and other third world people, primarily because God, rather than being viewed as liberator, was used as a dominating unmerciful oppressor who demanded submission from *His* subjects. Conveniently, of course, no real distinction was made between the heavenly Father/Master and the earthly father/master. Hence slaves were to give obedience to their earthly masters as unto Christ.

When theology gives support to a model of relationships based on domination and submission, the nature of humanity is severely distorted. Some feminists have emphasized the negative impact of this kind of dualism upon women. Women and other victims tend to be forced to the weak negative side of the social sexual dualism. Women are thereby perceived to be weak and submissive while men are viewed to be strong and dominant. In the realm of human interaction men function as God.[3] In the same vein, in a racist society, blacks are to be submissive while whites are dominant because the former are perceived to be inferior and the latter superior. This distorted view of humanity has tainted the contents of theology.

Recognizing this pattern in theological thinking, in 1969 the National Committee of Black Churchmen (later renamed National Committee of Black Christians) defined black theology in relation to black humanity.

> Black theology is a theology of Black liberation. It seeks to plumb the Black condition in the light of God's revelation in Jesus Christ, so that the Black community can see that the gospel is commensurate with the achievements of Black humanity. Black theology is a theology of "Blackness." It is the affirmation of Black humanity that emancipates Black people from white racism thus providing authentic freedom for both white people and Black people. It affirms the humanity of white people in that it says No to the encroachment of white oppression.[4]

This affirmation of black humanity does not negate white humanity—it merely rejects oppressive distortions about the nature of white people and black people.

Experience, Empowerment, and Theology

Denied humanity, ripped history, and stolen culture have meant that theologians invalidated the black experience by considering it as noncontributory to theology. The same is true of other disciplines such as history in which the black experience is considered, at best, to be a sub-cultural deviation. Black theology however, affirms the black experience as a primary source for theologizing. Much of this experience has involved pain and suffering caused by legal slavery and institutional racism.

When black theologians claim that the black experience is a critical source of theology, they finally legitimize the heritage of a people dehumanized for the purposes of exploitation. Their thoughts, music form, language form, and stories suddenly become important for an enterprise which had previously ignored them. Black theology takes these as its primary sources.

This newly affirmed heritage provides data for a new black expression in theology. The Bible is interpreted by blacks within the context of their experience of oppression. God identifies with people in modern times in captivity just as God identified with the people of Israel in captivity.

> Go down Moses,
> Way down in Egypt land.
> Tell old Pharaoh
> "Let my people go!"

The modern day pharaohs are no less sinful than those of biblical times and, therefore, God's identification with enslaved and oppressed black people is no less real. This divine identification manifested itself incarnationally. That explains Jesus' identification with the captives:

> The Spirit of the Lord is upon me, because he hath anointed me to preach the gospel to the poor; he hath sent me to heal the broken-hearted, to preach deliverance to the captives, and recovering of sight to the blind, to set at liberty them that are bruised.[5]

Jesus effectively solidifies and elevates the experiences of the weak, the downtrodden, the outcast. From this passage, two significant things happen: Jesus identifies himself with marginalized people; and the marginalized persons may discover that they are not bound by their current life-situation. Jesus' words serve as a source for the marginalized persons' realization—a necessary process for liberating oppressed peoples.

What stands out in black people's understanding of Jesus' proclamation and in the Bible generally, is that just as God sent Moses, Jesus, and other deliverers in the past, God continues to send deliverers in the present. Again, the confidence in God comes from the understanding that God, not racist white people, is the author of the humanity of black people.

Equally important is the sense of empowerment that comes from the affirmation of the black experience and the perception that Jesus identifies with victims. Though not often spoken of in such terms, theology and power have been directly related to each other throughout history. The theological establishment has often been in cahoots with the social, political, and economic status quo. One sees this as one reviews the history of the churches' defense of slavery (American slavery) and witchhunting (European and American).

Weak and victimized people are often annihilated by strong and powerful oppressors. The annihilation takes place on psychological, social, political, economic, and religious levels. These forces have worked together to create impoverished, disenfranchised, and impotent life situations for the victims. A World Council of Churches study makes clear that the victims of racism, including black Americans, have suffered in all of these areas.

> Almost every aspect of civilization—science, religion, law, economics, politics, etiquette, and art—has been infected with white racism. All the institutions in western culture, including the church, are inheritors of the racism which flourished for more than 300 years in Europe and America and continues today in many manifest and latent forms.[6]

One does not encounter racism only during some special rite of passage into life's larger community or at adulthood. Instead it pervades the whole experience of those who are its victims.

> Racism is present whenever persons, even before they are born, because of their race, are assigned to a group severely limited in their freedom of movement, their choice of work, their places of residence and so on.

> Racism is present whenever groups of people, because of their race, are denied effective participation in the political process, and so are compelled (often by force) to obey the edicts of governments which they were allowed to have no part in choosing.

> Racism is present whenever racial groups within a nation are excluded from the normal channels of educational opportunities and entry into occupational groups.

> Racism is present whenever the identity of persons is deni- grated through stereotyping of racial and ethnic groups in textbooks, cinema, mass media, interpersonal relations and other ways.[7]

Essentially, as this World Council of Churches statement affirms, even before their conception, black people have been doomed by the pervasiveness of racism.

Experience has always been a source for doing theology. The only question is, Whose experience? In fact, it has been the experience of those who have been writing theology—essentially white males. Their experience has been presented in a form so as to make the unsuspecting believe that it is the normative or universal experience. It is an experience of those conversant with the principalities and powers. It includes their perception of those who are different from them—non-white and non-male.

Theology has consequently been written from the topside of history. Views from the underside have come only in the form of reactionary, sometimes revolutionary activities of individuals and groups. In the black experience those revolutionary dissenters included folks like David Walker, Harriet Tubman, Sojourner Truth, Henry Highland Garnet, Nat Turner, Denmark Vesey, Henry McNeal Turner and groups like the Free African Society and the African Methodist Episcopal Church.

J. DeOtis Roberts, in an essay entitled "Black Theology in Dialogue: Two Examples," joins David Shannon, a biblical scholar and educator, in calling "Afro-Americans to become 'subjects' rather than 'objects' of history." He notes that people "who have been victimized and handicapped by a long history of oppression...will be defeated by circumstances" unless they change their futures. Certainly this task is easier said than done. Roberts, of course, recognizes that such an expectation "is difficult when one has suffered a depletion of material resources and psychological resources." And yet it is at the same time, "an essential posture for the underclasses in American society"[8] if their experience is to inform the task of doing theology.

The movement from object to subject is a movement in the process of empowerment. Black theology facilitates this movement. No longer is the white experience the set of spectacles through which we evaluate the black experience. The dominant culture does not provide the normative criteria for what makes up either culture or theology for those it may oppress.

Black theologians look at the black religious experience to discover the meaning of God's activities in the world today. Certainly God, our chief liberator, has little or no appeal for an oppressor who desires neither to reform or to be transformed. But for a people burdened with the shackles of past slavery and present institutional racism, God not only makes sense, but becomes a basic requirement for identification with the people. With this identification comes a *reaffirmed sense of somebodiness.* As the elders used to say, "the world didn't give it to me and the world can't take it away."

However, the critical question in considering youth ministry is, Can we assume the relevancy of theology to young people for whom ignorance of their own heritage precludes conscious identification with it? The lack of adequate education in the churches and secular institutions means that the past denial of black culture and history (especially in the schools) has fostered patterns of assimilationism. But to deny one's own heritage in the processes of assimilation into the dominant cultural experience yields the same consequences—displaced, disoriented, detached, angry, confused black youth.

The report of the Program to Combat Racism pointed out that racism affects even the unborn by defining the limitations of its victims prior to birth. These limitations continue throughout the development of children and young people. In his autobiographical film documentary, "Baldwin's Harlem," James Baldwin recalls his young readings of the black situation into which he was born and in which he watched his father deteriorate to a sense of impotence and hatred. He discerned how a racist society produces both self-hatred and hatred of whites in observations of the stark differences between "uptown" and "downtown" New York. Uptown was white, rich, and clean; downtown was black, poor, and dirty. Baldwin miraculously came out of the situation declaring "I'll die and go to hell before I let any white men sit on me—before I accept my place in this society." Thus he became a somebody. Too many black youth do die—physically (reflected in their high death rates); psychologically (through self-hatred and low motivation); or economically (through increasing unemployment leading to a permanent underclass).

Black theology contributes to our understanding of humanity by redefining the human in black form. That effort affirms the somebodiness of black people. It establishes the premises crucial to the development of a viable ministry for black youth.

On Becoming Human:
The Somebodiness of Black Youth

The title of a Saturday morning TV program, "Kids are People Too" is thought provoking; it critiques our general conception that children and youth are people in the making, not yet fully human.

In her feminist analysis of theological hierarchy, Sheila Collins speaks of the so-called biblical order of creation which tends to justify hierarchical human relationships. The order begins with God, followed by goodness, order, angels, Jesus, men, women, children, beasts, plants, earth, evil, and chaos. She focuses her attention on the inter-relationship among God, man, and woman. God creates and rules the world. Man rules woman who is beneath him. She, in turn, rules the children beneath her. It is interesting to note that children fall just above the beasts.

Obviously this ordering undergirds a particular line of authority. Just below the divine line we find man who holds the highest human authority. If we introduced a race analysis here, slaves and the children of slaves would probably fall below children.[9]   One can point to historical evidence that those who hold relatively lower human authority have at one time or another had their humanity debated.   The debate over whether or not women had souls happened centuries ago.   The debate over whether or not black and slave peoples had souls occurred more recently—within the past two centuries. Both women and slaves had been perceived to be property.   The Old Testament included them in the same property category (Deut. 5:21).   The constitution of the United States did not change the diminished status of either of these groups (notwithstanding the three-fifths compromise with respect to blacks).

It may follow then that children and youth, the objects of the authority of adults, would have their humanity challenged as well.   Certainly, they have been considered property.   The same "Are you human?" question raised with respect to blacks/slaves and women, can be raised with respect to young people.   Part of the tendency to negate the humanity of some peoples may be seen in the corresponding tendency to locate the blame for their situation on those who have been dehumanized.   Hence, we hear the familiar question: What is wrong with blacks or women or youth? What is their problem? Although these questions often have been asked, they are inappropiate questions.   The victims are blamed for situations and conditions over which they have no control.

One youth minister often expresses her frustration and disappointment with people who constantly ask her what is wrong with young people? She argues the problem may be with the adults who cannot see that youth are often society's victims.   These adults decry youth for engaging in illicit sex, and for using alcohol and drugs.

However, these adults do not give attention to limiting the millions of dollars spent by legitimate and illegitimate agencies that promote sex, alcohol and drugs. Youth are not the problem. Youth are the victims of adult inattention to the problems of youth.[10]

Negative judgments about youth are exacerbated in the society and church when compounded with the belief in what I call the "deferred church" syndrome. It is often expressed when youth are referred to as "the church of tomorrow" or "the future generation." They are never the people of today or the church of today. If we take seriously the present reality of youth and their church and community experiences, we must begin by re-thinking the meaning of their somebodiness theologically.

Perry LeFevre, in *Understandings of Man*, suggests three themes central to developing theories of humanity:

1. A theory of the human carries the assumption that something is wrong with human beings and usually an answer to the question, What is wrong with human beings?
2. It contains a normative judgment over what human ought to be. It describes the good *human being*.
3. It includes a way of moving from what is wrong with human beings to what the human is meant to be or what is fulfillment for the human.[11]

I assume something *is* wrong with humanity. White people have suffered from distorted hierarchical images of themselves, which led them to create destructive oppressive structures, legislating the goodness of white people while conveying black meant sin, darkness, evil, and ugliness.[12]

For blacks, America was, and to some extent still is, no place to be somebody. Blacks still suffer from the basic denial of human dignity reflected by the extent of their victimization by the social, economic, and political ills of our day. One of the turning points from this road of victimization was the civil rights/black power movement of the fifties, sixties, and seventies. For the first time in the United States blacks experienced what it meant to name themselves.

James Brown popularized it for both young and old— "Say it loud, I'm black and I'm proud." This affirmation of self had never been experienced from the larger society. The "black and proud" revolution undergirded the "manhood" movement of the same period which supported Eldridge Cleaver's proclamation that "we shall have our manhood. We shall have it or the earth will be leveled by our efforts to gain it." The leaders of these movements recognized, (as reflected in the National Committee of Black Christians' definition of black theology), that the primary issue had to do with the meaning of being human. The "nobody" status to which blacks were relegated by white racism was rejected in a loud and consistent way. "Say it loud," they sang with Brown, "I'm black and I'm proud."

The quest for human dignity had implications for all institutions of life. Blacks demanded equality in the job market. Programs of economic development were proposed, including the call for reparation.[13] Schools were challenged. Desegregation and integration were considered necessary since "separate but equal" did not guarantee equality. Out of the valleys of the shadow of death (called "ghettos"), came the shouts for decent and fair housing and the painful cries for adequate health care. Despite these efforts, however, the National Urban League report, *The State of Black America 1987*, revealed no significant long-standing progress has yet occurred in any of these areas.[14]

These forces come together to form the depressed and complex reality of black people in America—even today. The oppressive character of many institutions and policies may lead some still to ask, Are we human? When we consider the continuing dehumanization of the masses alongside the success of the few, it is possible to identify manydefects in these oppressive systems bent on creating races of nobodies. This is why Jesse Jackson has sought to help young people simply affirm their somebodiness. "I am somebody," he has them repeat:

> I am somebody!
> I may be poor,
> but I am somebody!

To be somebody is to be human. Black theology affirms the essential humanity of black people as a necessary step in the process of liberation. It is a step the church must take to engage in a liberating ministry to and for its youth.

George Thomas provides a helpful summary of the intention of a black theology of liberation. As a pan-Africanist, he draws upon the continuity between the African and the African-American experiences. He also articulates a holistic and global understanding of liberation that establishes the framework for affirming black humanity.

1. To reclaim and restore the positive legacy of the black experience as continuous from the African into the American context.
2. To demythologize those religious and non-religious anti-black and anti-poor conceptions and perspectives which demean African, black and poor, oppressed humanity.

3. To engage the liberation struggle of all oppressed peoples against the concepts, structures, and systems that assault human dignity.

4. To press the black church and community into the wider society of America and the world to be prophetic and political in the witness and action for socio-economic justice.

5. To share in the ultimate transformation of the human life styles in every place for the coming of the global village and the new world community.[15]

In this summary, the somebodiness of black people is affirmed. It reclaims our connection to the past, recognizes the reality of our present situation, and expands our vision toward the global community. To counteract the negative images impressed upon the minds of youth, black theology restores the positive legacy of black people. Black theology rids the mind of the anti-black sentiments that James Baldwin described as his context for growing up. To rid ourselves and our community of destructive behavior (drugs, alcohol, self-hatred), black theology leads the people to engage in liberating actions emphasizing social, political and economic justice. The aim of black theology is to change not only the lives of poor black Americans, but the lives of the oppressed everywhere.

Implications for the Church and Its Ministry to Youth

While a black theology affirms the humanity of blacks in general, I would argue that special attention must be given to the humanity of youth. Black theologians must be willing to examine and challenge the church's assumptions about youth. As I reflect upon LeFevre's themes in any theory of humanity, I am prepared to make the following confession of my assumptions:

1. *Black young people are not in process of becoming human; they are indeed human.* They may be in the process of intellectual, psychological, and physical development, but they are no less human.

2. *Something is wrong with black youth.* That error cannot be adequately analyzed in isolation from the reality of living in a racist, sexist, classist, imperialistic, militaristic, ageist society. Black youth are often merely victims of their circumstances. In other words, something is really wrong with the larger society, and that something is manifested in the particular experiences of young people.

3. *Black youth ought to be black youth.* They ought not try to be (like) white youth. In fact they ought not even try to be adults—black or white—though some are plunged into early adulthood because of the demands of poverty existence. But they must affirm who they are as they make that critical group identification with black people.

If the church could accept these three principles, several effective results could serve as recommendations for the church's ministry to youth.

1. The black church needs to develop sufficent facilities and skills to systematically analyze youth experiences. The data from such an analysis provides the impetus for prophetic and political responsibility crucial to black liberation. Because young people do not exist in a vacuum, their lives cannot be analyzed in a vacuum. Instead a careful systematic study would create a more accurate understanding of the world and experiences of black youth. This study would involve, for example, attention to the inadequate education most receive.

Perhaps no one has criticized the American educational system for its impact upon black people as clearly as Carter G. Woodson did more than fifty years ago in his classic *The Mis-Education of the Negro*. Blacks, he argued, are taught to despise who they are so much that they are often alienated from their own communities.[16] Several decades later, in *Death at an Early Age*, Jonathan Kozol carefully analyzed textbooks to discover the extent to which negative judgments regarding non-white, non-dominant culture persons have continued to be implanted in the minds of children.[17] Kozol found for example, that "the people of South Africa have one of the most democratic governments now in existence in any country"; that "white managers" were needed in Africa at the time "to show the Negroes how to work and to manage the plantations"; and that "the Negro is very quick to imitate and follow the white man's way of living...."[18] Kozol's attention to detail illustrates the kind of critical analysis black churches should be giving to the images conveyed by the dominant insitutions.

The public school system loses black children at an early age. To counter that loss churches need to identify the ways schools and other agencies oppress and limit the experiences and possibilities of black children and youth. This task is political and prophetic because it focuses on bringing black youth from the periphery to the center of the education system. Morever, a systemic analysis may contribute to the transformation of the education of black children and youth for the promotion of their sense of somebodiness.

2. The black church must continue to produce its own theology. The black church can no longer give up its theological growth and development to white people. Theology as I indicated is *done* in the context of experience. Black experience is alien to white people (interestingly in a way that the white experience is not alien to black people). The black church must produce its own scholars to do its own theology. This will not be a totally new endeavor.

We have a history of doing our own theology. When Richard Allen walked out of St. George Methodist Episcopal Church to establish a congregation for blacks in Philadelphia, it was not only a sociological statement; it was a theological statement as well. Our God, he was saying, is a just God. Some scholars have argued that there is no theological difference between black and white Methodists. They fail to realize, however, that before it became popular for contemporary theologians to talk about praxis, black church folks had been engaged in it for almost two centuries. When Allen left white-dominated church life, his act involved more than social protest. It revealed the expectations of a liberating and just God. Similar activities by the Free African Society, the early black church, and religious personalities further illustrate a black liberating praxis of a people serving a just and liberating God.

We must, therefore, continue to train those persons designated to unveil this theological history and to interpret the contemporary work of the church. This task does not belong to the theological school alone. It begins in the congregation as pastors and teachers take teaching black youth seriously. The content of that teaching encompasses the tradition of Christian faith and the black experience. It calls for familiarity on the part of youth with both the content of those traditions and the skills to use that content to comprehend their present situation and circumstance. It leads to the establishing programs of black religious study to help black youth obtain the resources and develop the skills to live out their own liberation.

3. As we develop our religious scholars and leadership, the black church must also develop its own curriculum resources. The significance of this third recommendation was underscored for me by my seminary professor, the Reverend Homer McEwen. He told the story of a Sunday school class in a black church. As the group moved to the lesson's questions for discussion, they found this question, "What would you do if a black person were to walk into this class?" After a brief pause, followed by some laughter, someone concluded, "Well, the book obviously was written for a white church and for white people."

As in the secular educational system, most Christian education materials have been designed primarily to give validity and support to whites, thereby affirming white culture as normative and good, invalidating blacks by denigrating black culture as nonexistent, bad, or evil. This has been most evident in the careless use of color symbolism in church resources—identifying white with good and black with evil or bad. White has been used to symbolize God and Jesus Christ and the good in humanity.[19]

My argument is that the problems with black youth ministry are essentially theological problems. The issues relate to the doctrine of humanity: racism and ageism. Black churches need to broaden the struggle for human dignity to embrace the concerns and needs of black youths. In a culture that yearns for youth yet holds little respect for them, black youth are doubly victimized. Consequently, the church must reinforce and celebrate the fact that black youth are people too.

─────── *NOTES* ───────

1. Owen Thomas, *Introduction to Theology* (Wilton, Conn.: Morehouse-Barlow Co., Inc., 1983), Introduction passim.

2. James Cone, *A Black Theology of Liberation* (New York: J. B. Lippincott, 1970), p. 17.

3. For discussions of these patriarchal understandings of women, see Sheila Collins, *A Different Heaven and Earth* (Valley Forge, Pa.: Judson Press, 1974; Elizabeth Dodson Gray, *Green Paradise Lost* (Wellesley, Mass.: Roundtable Press, 1979); Virginia Mollencott, *Women, Men, and the Bible* (Nashville: Abingdon, 1977).

4. The National Committee of Black Churchmen, "Black Theology," in *Black Theology: A Documentary History, 1966-1979*, eds. Gayraud Wilmore and James Cone (New York: Orbis Books, 1979), pp. 100-02.

5. Luke 4:18.

6. The Commission on Faith and Order and the Programme to Combat Racism, *Racism in Theology—Theology Against Racism* (Geneva: World Council of Churches, 1975), p. 6.

7. *Ibid.*, 6-7.

8. J. DeOtis Roberts, *Black Theology in Dialogue* (Philadelphia: Westminster Press, 1987), pp. 106-07, 157.

9. This is probably why during slavery even a six-year-old girl would be "Miss Ann" to an adult slave, even though to her an adult slave would be merely auntie, uncle, Tom, Jane, boy, or girl.

10. Conversations with Debora Grant, youth minister at Flipper Temple A.M.E. Church, Atlanta, Georgia.

11. Perry LeFevre, *Understandings of Man* (Philadelphia: Westminster Press, 1966), p. 27.

12. Eulalio Balthazar, *The Dark Center* (New York: Paulist Press, 1973), Passim.

13. "The Black Manifesto", *Black Theology: A Documentary History, 1966-1979*, eds. Gayraud S. Wilmore and James H. Cone (New York: Orbis Books, 1979), pp. 80-9.

14. In spite of this, the condition of blacks remains deprived. See the National Urban League Report, *The State of Black America 1987* (New York: National Urban League, 1987).

15. George Thomas, "Black Theology of Liberation," *The Journal of the Inter-denominational Center*, VII (Fall 1979), pp. 43-4.

16. Carter G. Woodson, *The Mis-education of the Negro* (Philadelphia: Hakim's Publications, 1933), Passim.

17. Jonathan Kozol, *Death at an Early Age* (Houghton Mifflin Co., 1967. Excerpts printed in *America's Other Youth: Growing Up Poor* by David Gottlieb and Anne Lienherd Heinsohn (Englewood Cliffs, N.J.: Prentice-Hall, 1971).

18. *Ibid., America's Other Youth*, 185.

19. For a discussion of color symbolism, see Balthazar, *The Dark Center* and Gayraud Wilmore, "Black Messiah: Revising the Color Symbolism of Western Christology," *The Journal of the Interdenominational Theological Center*, II (Fall 1974), pp. 8-18.

CHAPTER FOUR

Retrieving Intergenerational and Intercultural Faith

ROMNEY M. MOSELEY

Editor's introduction: Literature on African American youth rarely attends to the social meanings of their experience. Romney Moseley's essay begins to fill this gap. He draws a composite picture of African American youth as they live out their experiences in the larger American and Black American society. This overview leads Moseley to explore several implications for the future direction of black youth ministries. He focuses on the retrieval of the intergenerational faith that has historically distinguished the black religious experience, the development of what he calls transforming leaders among black youth, and the engagement of black youth through the church's ministry with the global and intercultural issues affecting their own futures.

*A*ttention to the church's ministry to black youth comes at a time when recent studies indicate that the future does not bode well for them. Unemployment, drugs, teenage pregnancy and dropping out of school are some of their most serious problems. Sociologist Andrew Billingsley reports that:

> From a high of 24.4 percent in 1960, unemployment in this group actually fluctuated upward and landed back at 24 percent by the end of the decade before soaring again to a high of 35.4 percent in 1980 and to an astronomical 40 percent by 1982, which remained steady through 1985. As a consequence, there are hundreds of thousands of

black youth between 18 and 25 years of age who have never had a full-time job and are destined never to have one. When the "discouraged" workers are considered, the number out of work nearly doubles.[1]

Unemployment is especially disturbing considering the fact that low-income households headed by single women are becoming the norm for black families. In 1960, 78 percent of black families were married couples. By 1985, as a result of increases in the divorce rate, in the number of young black men in prisons over those in college, in the mortality rate of black men, and in unmarried parenthood, 44 percent of black families were headed by single females. In contrast, 13 percent of white families are headed by single women. Furthermore, in 1986, 43 percent of black youth under age 18 lived in poverty, compared to 16 percent of white children. Studies indicate that families headed by a single mother under 25 are most likely impoverished. This is especially serious for black families. Then there is the nagging problem of teenage pregnancy.

Each year more than a million American teenagers become pregnant. Four out of five of them are unmarried. Some 30,000 of those who become pregnant are under age thirteen. Both the pregnancy and birth rates for black teens are over four times higher than among white teens. Black adolescents also begin childbearing at younger ages than whites, increasing the likelihood of subsequent births during teenage years. If present trends continue, researchers estimate that 40 percent of today's 14-year-old girls will be pregnant at least once before the age of twenty.

If that trend is anywhere close to accurate for the general populations, it is frightful to imagine the percentages of black teenagers that will be affected. While the cost

of these pregnancies for the nation exceeds $16.6 billion
annually in social, welfare, and administrative services, the
loss in human potential is incalculable. While the black
girls are having babies, increasingly young black men have
dropped out of school, deserted to careers in crime.
Taken together, the pregnancy rates of young black females and the "social drop-out" rates among black males
pose real threats to the hope of a stable black community.
But it is this lack of hope, not potential, which is most
debilitating for today's black youth.[2]

Added to this litany of social ills is the perennial problem of education. The majority of black youth are still
"at risk" in public schools that are *de facto* segregated. This
situation will undoubtedly worsen by the end of this
century when one-third of the nation's population will
most likely be non-white. Meanwhile black academic
achievement remains below that of their white counterparts, especially in the inner city districts. This situation
is aggravated by inferior educational resources and the
persistent condition of segregation in which more than
two-thirds of black youth are educated. While the drop-
out problem cuts across all ethnic and geographical
boundaries, it is most acute in the inner cities among poor
ethnic youth where the dropout rate is three times that of
affluent youth.

These perennial social problems have always been the
concern of the black church. However, the church is not
an invincible bastion immune to the social ills facing black
society. Chronic racism, segregation, unemployment and
the increasing "underclass" of perennially poor, unedu-
cated black youth, most of whom live in single-parent
households in the inner cities constitute a dominant
segment of the social infrastructure of the black church.

Black Americans can ill afford to dwell on the gains of

the Civil Rights struggles of the fifties and sixties as the definitive norm of black society. While many blacks were able to move upward socially and economically, this is not true for the majority of blacks. Moreover, the economic gains of the civil rights movement mainly benefited blacks who were already in the middle class.

The visibility of the black middle class might detract attention from the pressing economic hardships facing most blacks. This is particularly evident in the case of blacks who have moved into higher-status historically and predominantly white denominations and churches that attract a large following of success-seekers from across ethnic lines. These churches offer well-organized pastoral counseling services, youth ministries, academic tutoring, support groups for addicts and their families, and audio and video programs to inspire an indominable combination of spiritual growth and economic success.

Some black churches provide similar services. Without their assistance in providing childcare for working parents, afterschool care, and remedial education through tutoring and intervention programs such as Headstart, the statistics on black dropouts from school, academic failure and teenage pregnancy would most likely be far worse. Fortunately, in the past decade, many black church leaders realized that the magnitude of social problems required an ecumenical approach. The rhetoric of black theology that characterized the National Committee of Black Churchmen (later changed to more enlightened nomenclature, the National Committee of Black Christians) was superceded by a more pragmatic Congress of National Black Churches (CNBC).

Founded in 1975 by Bishop John Hurst Adams of the African Methodist Episcopal Church (AME), the CNBC is comprised of five of the seven historically black denominations in the United States.[3] This organization has produced one of the most significant and genuinely ecumenical programs to assist black youth, namely, Project SPIRIT—an acronym for strengths, perseverance, imagination, responsibility, integrity and talent. This program nurtures the personal, moral, spiritual and educational formation of black youth. The CNBC also sponsors an Anti-Drug Abuse Campaign that is funded by the United States Department of Justice. This project assists churches and communities in 25 cities throughout the United States in their efforts to dissuade black youth from falling into the bottomless pit of drug abuse.[4] Two other programs assisting black youth may be found in Chicago. They include the Christian Heritage Center led by the Rev. Mary Carr and SEED (a program for educational and economic development) led by the Rev. James Bevel.

Throughout the country, black churches are involved in systematic efforts to preserve the integrity of the black family. These include the Black Youth Project of the Family Life Center founded by the Shiloh Baptist Church in Washington, D.C.; The Living Consortium—a program of Abyssinian, Canaan and Memorial Baptist churches sponsored by the Urban League of New York; and Project Image in Chicago—a project of ten churches that focuses on black male identity formation. Other programs are sponsored by the Concord Baptist Church in Brooklyn, New York; Allen Temple Baptist Church in Oakland, California; Pilgrim's Hope Baptist Church in Los Angeles; People Baptist Church in Boston; Allen A.M.E. Church in Jamaica, New York; Ebenezer and Wheat Street Baptist Churches in Atlanta; Bethel A.M.E. Church in Atlanta; and Hartford Baptist Church in Detroit.

Despite these and other valiant efforts to stem the erosion of the black family, a major issue facing the black church is its ability to resist fragmentation along class lines. During the Reagan years, a few blacks benefited substantially from the aura of peace and prosperity. Their visibility is duly recorded in articles and books on the "new black middle class" and the "new black elite."[5] With the flight of middle-class blacks into the suburbs and the loss of industrial jobs in the inner cities, inner city schools, churches, and businesses that once served blacks from all classes were left to "the truly disadvantaged."[6]

The black church therefore has to generate youth leadership that cuts across class lines. This is easier said than done. In this country, leadership is shaped by the demands of technological and financial productivity. The temptation to ignore pressing problems of social justice in favor of accommodating to the possibilities and rewards of upward social mobility is particularly strong among middle-class blacks. The magnetism of triumphal religion with its privatization of piety and instrumental understanding of Christian faith as a medium of economic and political success appeals to blacks who see themselves at the vanguard of the new black elite. Bouyed by triumphal religion and advanced capitalism, black urban professionals (buppies) are increasingly prominent in quasi-religious organizations whose promises of financial success are couched in the language of divine fulfillment.

Therefore, the black church finds itself with the problem of fostering positive images of success and productivity for its youth while maintaining its historic commitment to social justice. It cannot be content to cultivate a new black elite as the matrix of social transformation. Any attempt to create a cordon of middle class blacks is subversive. It undermines the tradition of the extended family by which blacks exercise reciprocal obligations across distinctions of class and transmit faith from one generation to another. No studies of intergenerational faith in the histories of black families are available to document its importance.

The survival of America's black youth depends on the protection of the extended family and the bridging of boundaries of class and caste. Billingsley indicates that "the extended family pattern is not just a structural coping tactic but has evolved into a strong valuable cultural pattern."[7] He also disputes the argument that "underclass" blacks and the "black elite" do not share the same moral virtues and values. According to Billingsley, "the poor have the same basic American values of stability, achievement, and upward mobility that other Americans have. It is their inability to attain these values that distinguishes them from the others, and this inability is a highly structured feature of the society at large."[8] Thus he rejects the assertion that the black middle class is responsible for the creation and plight of the "underclass" in the urban ghettos.[9] The truth is that the black middle class exists in a rather precarious position in American society.

> In a number of major respects, the black middle class is more vulnerable to the threat of downward mobility than the more established white middle class....In addition to the challenge of moving into more secure and independent occupations and accumulating family wealth, black families face a third challenge—transmitting their status and economic well-being to their children. Large numbers of middle-class black families are finding that they have not prepared their children to succeed them or to stand on their shoulders. As a consequence, many families may lose the upward mobility drive which has characterized them since before the end of American slavery.[10]

The precariousness of the black middle class compounds the critical situation of black family life in America. Yet, I suspect that the success of the black middle class is becoming the dominant ideology in the programs for identity formation and leadership development of black youth. Some prominent black churches hold this world view. However, to avoid further fragmentation of black America along class lines, the black church must adopt a clearly defined and pragmatic theological hermeneutic to guide its ministries.

Evidently, the prophetic imagination of black theology that galvanized the black church of the sixties and early seventies has exhausted its momentum. With the exception of the Black Theology Project, black theology has failed to have any significant impact as a practical approach of social transformation. This approach must be grounded in the interdependence of scripture and the daily experience of black Americans to illumine the meaning of life.

Evidently, the prophetic imagination of black theology that galvanized the black churches of the sixties and early seventies has exhausted its momentum. With the exception of the Black Theology Project, black theology has failed to have any significant impact as a practical guide to social transformation. Its prophetic power languishes in theological seminaries alongside other forms of "transformative" religion popular in the sixties and seventies. As one recent critic observes, black theology has evolved from being a popular theology to "an object of scientific study, something about which people hold conferences, write books, and give lectures."[11] Its impact on black youth is questionable. This is indeed unfortunate since black theology emerged on the intellectual scene as a powerful paradigm of theological reconstruction allied to similar ventures in social reconstruction generated by the quest for black power and black identity formation. Together, these ventures provided black youth with the theological and political ideas for disembedding themselves from the shackles of segregation and inferiority.

But we are in a new era of social and theological construction. New metaphors and models of ministry to black youth are necessary in order to provide leadership for the next century.

Transactional and Transforming Leadership

Political scientist James McGregor Burns suggests that the principle distinguishing feature of leadership has to do with the intended purpose. Leadership is an act of power but its purpose is to induce followers

> to act for certain goals that represent the values and the motivations—the wants and needs, the aspirations and expectations—of both *leaders* and *followers*. And the genius of leadership lies in the manner in which leaders see and act on their own and their followers' values and motivations. Leadership unlike power-wielding, is thus inseparable from followers' needs and goals. The essence of the leader-follower relation is the interaction of different persons with different levels of motivation and of power potential, including skill, in pursuit of a common purpose.[12]

Power, on the other hand, is a relationship between power-wielders and recipients. But unlike leadership, the purpose of power is the attainment of the power-wielder's goals which "may be relevant to the *recipient's* needs only as necessary to exploit them."[13]

The genius of Martin Luther King, Jr.'s leadership lay in this ability to utilize non-violent resistance as a means of uniting both leaders and followers behind a common *telos* of social justice and freedom, values that are ends in themselves. Such is the nature of *transforming* leadership. According to Burns, this form of leadership occurs "when one or more persons *engage* with others in such a way that leaders and followers raise one another to higher levels in motivation and morality."[14]

In contrast, the more common type of leadership, *transactional* leadership occurs

> when one person takes the initiative in making contact with others for the purpose of an exchange of valued things. Their purposes are related, at least to the extent that the purposes stand within the bargaining process and can be advanced by maintaining that process. But beyond this the relationship does not go. The bargainers have no enduring purpose that holds them together; hence they may go their separate ways. A leadership act took place, but it was one that binds leader and follower together in a mutual and continuing pursuit of a higher purpose.[15]

It should be noted that transforming and transactional leadership are not mutually exclusive. Martin Luther King, Jr. was also an astute transactional leader in bargaining for the material and political needs of his people. Similarly, the various programs and projects on ministry to youth mentioned earlier issue from a firm matrix of transactional leadership. In order to address the complex problems facing black youth, churches have to exercise both forms of leadership.

Black Ecumenical Leadership

If the black church is to effectively develop youth leadership, it must adopt a strong ecumenical identity.

This has been a major problem for the black church. The National Congress of Black Churches, the Interdenominational Theological Center, and Partners in Ecumenism are important agents of ecumenical consciousness. But more needs to be done. Here the National Council of Churches and the World Council of Churches are invaluable.

Only in recent years has the World Council of Churches paid any attention to the plight of black religious life in the United States. Documents from the first world conference of Christian youth held in Amsterdam in 1939 and subsequent meetings in Oslo in 1947 indicate the absence of black American youth. In 1948, a delegation of one hundred youth attended the First Assembly of the World Council of Churches in Amsterdam. The records do not mention anything about the presence of black American youth. More importantly, a Youth Depart-ment established by the World Council of Churches, became actively involved in the post-war reconstruction of Europe and training courses organized at the Ecumenical Institute at Bossey. Hans van der Bent reports that:

> Eastern Europe in its ideological isolation became a focus of direct regular activity; the concerns for creative youth work in Latin America and Asia, and later in Africa and the Middle East, were explored. *A truly international outlook characterized the work of the Youth Department.* (emphasis added).[16]

The scope is truly international, but what about America's black youth? It is conceivable that the forces of segregation negated any involvement of American blacks in these ecumenical ventures. In 1951, the Central Committee of the WCC meeting at Rolle, Switzerland, proclaimed that the church's ministry to powerless and persecuted churches "had to be achieved through and with the participation of the young generation in its own ecumenical context."[17] Later in 1954, at the WCC General Assembly in Evanston, Illinois, the Youth Department adopted the theme of "The Integration of Youth in the Life and Mission of the Church" and promised "to keep before the churches their responsibility for the evangelization of young people and their growth in the Christian faith."[18] Nothing indicates that America's black youth were represented at this assembly. It should be underscored that this was the very year that the U. S. Supreme Court struck down the laws that legitimated segregation in the public schools. Evidently, America's black youth were not only victims of America's national sin but were also ignored by the world church.

The political awareness of youth reached its zenith fourteen years later at the WCC General Assembly in Uppsala, Sweden in 1968, shortly after the death of Martin Luther King, Jr. Prompted mainly by this tragedy, the youth participants focused on the issues of racism and oppression throughout the world. Today, these concerns continue to be addressed by European youth. The annual *Kirchentage* in West Germany, for example, gathers more than 250,000 Protestants, most of whom are under 25, who voice the major concerns of peace, ecology, and global solidarity against oppression. This gathering has no equivalent in the United States, and certainly not among black youth.

Retrieving Intergenerational Faith

The contemporary social situation demands that the church retrieve its militant heritage as an arena for dialogue on any moral, political, economic, and spiritual issues confronting black identity formation. No other institution is equipped to be the locus of authority, the cradle of transforming leadership, and the matrix of symbols and rituals essential to the creation of structures for making meaning for our youth. Black youth will not be merely content with projects and programs that are limited to the utilitarian bartering of transactional leadership, however successful these are as a bulwark against the disintegration of the black family.

Unfortunately, racism's historic roots are so embedded in American culture that black church efforts are minimal in generating leadership that transcends the bargaining and bartering postures of transactional leadership. Moving beyond these postures requires a sense of identity that recapitulates the ancestral cultural and religious heritage of African Americans. This means that on the local and international levels ecumenism must be a priority for the black church. Already embattled by a litany of social evils, America's black youth can ill afford further isolation from the efforts of the global church to stand in solidarity with the oppressed.

Reconnecting black youth to their ancestral heritage and transmitting intergenerational faith is the responsibility of the black church. Church leaders must expect resistance from blacks who believe that they have reached the pinnacle of success in America. Resistance will also come from governmental authorities threatened by any efforts on the part of blacks to establish solidarity with emancipatory movements in the African diaspora. The old imperialist strategy of *dividere et imperare* (divide and rule) that has proven effective in keeping blacks throughout the world in subjugation is alive and well.

Even during the liberal administration of President Jimmy Carter, a document has been disclosed recom-

mending the sharpening of social stratification in the
black community in order to widen and perpetuate the
gap between successful educated blacks and the poor.
The intent was to frustrate the formation of movements
representing different social strata in the black community and to prevent the emergence of black leadership
that would appeal nationally to blacks from across social
boundaries. Despite these efforts, Jesse Jackson emerged
as such a leader in two election campaigns for the presi-
dency of the United States. Though he did not win the
nomination of the Democratic Party, Jackson was successful in attracting a large broad-based and multi-ethnic
constituency from all socio-economic classes. Jackson was
not simply a role model for blacks. Neither was he
symbolic leader chosen by whites as a spokesman for
blacks. His second political campaign was a genuine
exercise in transforming leadership.

The fact a black pastor-politician could generate such
support augers well for the moral and spiritual reconstruction of American society. Jackson preached a simple
message "Down with dope! Up with hope!" that struck at
the heart of a fundamental issue paralyzing black youth.
While it is not enough to dwell on slogans, it is important
to recognize their metaphorical value. Black youth need
to be carried beyond the ravages of the drug culture and
the fragmentation of the black family. The challenge to
the church is to find new metaphors to halt the cycle of
violence and victimization among black youth.

Michael Warren suggests the following four vectors of
ministry that are relevant to the needs of black youth:

> The ministry of the word, that is the meanings that bind
> the community together as they confront their current
> situation in the world; the ministry of worship, that is, the
> community's celebration of its common understandings

and of the bonds they create; the ministry of guidance and counsel, including education; and the ministry of healing both to its own members and to a world seriously out of step with its own vision of human existence.[19]

Of primary importance is the ministry of the word—the meanings that bind the black community together as it faces the contemporary world.   Black Americans are a people with "core beliefs."[20] The history of black America is a history of suffering, oppression, and the will to survive. For black Christians, their history recapitulates the "dangerous memory" of the suffering, death, and resurrection of Jesus Christ. And so black Christians stand in solidarity with victims of oppression and witness with them as a community of hope. The civil rights era and the pressing concerns of today have shown that this hope can no longer be embedded in a naive otherworldliness but should be sharply articulated in terms of an emancipatory praxis.

The ambiguous separation of church and state in this nation places the onus on the church to retrieve and transmit to youth the narratives of suffering and freedom that constitute the soul of black identity. Without these narratives, black youth will flounder in the sea of identity confusion and be paralyzed by *anomie.* Michael Warren's assessment is correct.   The transmission of these meanings is not merely a matter of education but involves the total ministry of the church. The church is "an intergenerational community modeling active commitment to justice out of religious faith."

The vocation of the black church is to transmit this commitment to justice, and to solidify its foundations in a divine source of meaning and power intergenerationally, so that the dreams of the ancestors become the visions of the young. This requires education but also "active engagement"[21] with the values of freedom, justice, and human dignity that have shaped the history of our people. If not in the church, where will youth find mentors in grandparents and foster grandparents in whose souls the wisdom of our ancestors are indelibly written? The church is the last vestige of the extended black family and the principal resource for enlightening and strengthening the moral and spiritual development of black youth.

Secondly, we must attend to the ministry of worship. It is a truism that the black church is a worshipping community. From the storefront churches to the loftiest tabernacles, the slave songs, spirituals, and songs of force proclaim the agony of singing the Lord's songs in a strange land. In worship, the moral ordering of political life and the integration of personality are interrelated. Together they are born from faith in a covenant relationship with a providential God. Hence worship can never be eroded by harsh social and political realities such as those already cited. The dialectic of eternal presence and temporal existence is the bedrock of faith. Yet, despite the legendary spirituality of the black church, our youth have been deprived of opportunities to participate in the church's worship on national and international ecumenical levels. The time is ripe to move beyond the local church as the sole forum for celebrating common understandings of the community of faith.

Thirdly, we must emphasize the ministry of guidance, counsel, and education. In addition to the remedial education programs and counseling support systems provided for youth by black churches, the problem of identity formation exists. Erik Erikson reminds us that

> religion through the centuries has served to restore a sense of trust at regular intervals in the form of faith while giving tangible form to a sense of evil which it promises to

ban....Whosoever says he [sic] has religion must derive a faith from it which is transmitted to infants in the form of basic trust; whoever claims that he does not need religion must derive such basic faith from elsewhere.[22]

The basic trust heralded by Erikson is also claimed by James Fowler as "primal faith" from which emerges "intuitive-projective faith."[23]

A thorough description of Fowler's stages is beyond the scope of this essay. However, it is helpful to note the patterns of development relevant to youth. The classics of the tradition that are transmitted intergenerationally from the bedrock of what youth apprehend as trustworthy, true, and valuable have been noted. According to Fowler, in the early childhood years these narratives constitute the content of "mythic-literal faith." At this stage, the family's witness to the stories of biblical faith is paramount. Within the family and worshipping community, faith is mediated covenantally. Thus a salient feature of the church's ministry is to educate, literally to draw out, the deep structure or grammar of faith— the giving of the heart to the One whose love and faithfulness constitute the matrix of Christian hope and identity.

For older children, the stage of "synthetic-conventional faith" depicts the nexus of relationships with significant others whose interpretation of the received tradition defines the parameters of belonging to the community of faith. Here membership in the church is critical. While we would readily agree that worship in the black church tradition is a passionate and spiritually exhilarating experience, the church's invitation to youth to be "born again" is short-lived if it is proclaimed as an instantaneous conversion experience. This simply encourages pastors to ignore or minimize the more arduous task of nurturing the transformation and development of faith. Conversion experiences alone cannot be the bonding between youth and the community of faith. They need more to empower them to discover meaning in the face of the harsh realities of racism, unemployment, and the fragmentation of family life. Moreover, black youth are already saturated with a plethora of momentary ecstasy.

The next stage, "individuative-reflexive faith" underscores the task of fostering independence—not individualism. Dependence, independence, and interdependence are dialectically related. Whether adults like it or not, youth will formulate their own worldview in order to establish a vital sense of autonomy, and often it may be radically opposite to that of parents. This self-chosen shaping of the world characteristic reflects the American spirit of exploration and adventure. It also presupposes Erikson's "psychosocial moratorium"—a period of wanderlust and freedom. The latter does not portray the experience of black youth. In light of the socio-political and economic realities noted earlier, the transition to "individuative-reflexive faith" cannot be taken for granted. At this point, the history of suffering among blacks interrupts the easy progress of developmental theories.

At the same time, the contemporary situation demands that black pastors abandon the panacea of otherworldly preaching and assist black youth in the difficult task of individuation, that is, the task of becoming selves before God in a society that is fragmented by racism and which refuses to accept more than partial and superficial expressions of their humanity. Only the church is equipped with the resources for helping black youth to engage the paradox of suffering and liberation as they weave a tapestry of Christian faith in the face of the smouldering cinders of racism.

Finally, the ministry of healing. The concerns expressed in this essay imply that the status quo of black churches and white churches is unchangeable, perhaps eternally. Some might wonder why the "integration" of black and white churches in order to consolidate an effective ministry to black youth is not suggested. As a metaphor of social transformation, integration brought us beyond where we were prior to the civil rights era, but its usefulness has been exhausted. Now we need more appropriate metaphors of healing. Metaphors are paradoxical in that they define specific limits of understanding while bearing a surplus of meaning. As Sally McFague notes, "metaphor always has the character of is and is not."[24] In other words, we should understand that metaphors are tentative and, therefore, they demand that we be open to new transformations of consciousness.

At the risk of being utterly simplistic, I propose that the time has come for the black church to retrieve the metaphor of *oikumene.* I am not referring to interdenominational bureaucracies as a corrective to territorial defensiveness, competition for membership, financial empire-building, and the monopolization of power—all of which are endemic within black and white churches. Under these circumstances, ecumenism is impossible.

Kosuke Koyama reminds us that "the word *oikumene* is related to the word *oikos,* meaning house. The theology of *oikumene* challenges us to see the whole world as the "house of God."[25] As members of the household of God, black youth need to experience solidarity with victims of suffering that transcends national and ethnic boundaries. As the body of Christ, the church bears this anamnestic solidarity. Black youth in America should be witnesses to this solidarity throughout the world. Their voices need to be heard in the Youth Department of the World Council of Churches, in its conferences and General Assemblies.

They need to be participants in seminars at the Ecumenical Institute at Bossey, Switzerland and in cultural exchanges with other youth from around the globe.

In the United States, these programs tend to be restricted to white affluent students. But these intercultural relationships educate black youth for critical consciousness. Here they discover the interconnectedness of global power relationships and their relevance to structural poverty in black America and in the so-called third world. In these contexts, the struggle for justice, peace, and the appropriate care of the earth is more inclusive.

In conclusion, the contemporary socio-economic situation in America places an increasingly heavy burden on the church to revive the spirit of *oikumene* that empowered the emancipatory praxis of the church during the civil rights movement. This time the agenda calls for intercultural linkages with persons in the world church who are dramatically transforming the doing of theology. These are the voices of the non-European and non-North American poor who constitute the emerging majority of Christians living in the southern hemisphere.

Here the consciousness of youth in the base communities of Latin America leads them to relate theological interpretation directly to the action of God among the oppressed. In proclaiming God's "preferential option for the poor," these Christians underscore the reality of their history as the history of suffering and salvation. The emancipatory themes present in this discourse radically interrupts the progressive theologies of the rich industrial nations and challenges the excessive victories of triumphal religion. The black church can bring to this global conversation the vital faith of generations that have shared in the Christian story, thereby supplementing the faith education of youth mediated by family and school. Given the "at risk" status of both family and school, the church dare not retreat from its vocation.

My vision of the church's ministry to youth may be termed a practical theology of ministry. In the contemporary debate over what is meant by practical theology, I am influenced by my colleague, Charles Gerkin's "narrative hermeneutical perspective." I alluded to this perspective in advocating the retrieval of intergenerational faith. According to Gerkin,

> Practical theology, seen from a narrative hermeneutical perspective, involves a process of the interpretive fusion of horizons of meaning embodied in the Christian narrative with other horizons that inform and shape perceptions in which Christians participate.[26]

Gerkin adopts Hans-Georg Gadamer's concept of the "fusion of horizons" to capture the dialogical action of interpretation. In a culture that is permeated by racism, the horizons of black youth experience that inform and shape their perceptions are fraught with conflict and alienation. A practical theology of ministry to black youth has to be responsive to the multiple horizons of meaning that are present in black culture; it must recognize the persistent threats to meaning brought by racism, economic injustice, inferior education, and fragmentation of the family.

The precariousness of the contemporary social situation demands that the church—the *oikos* or household of God—make every effort to maintain a positive environment where youth are mentored in constructive leader-follower relationships and the virtues of wisdom, hope, and faith of the black historical experience are transmitted from generation to generation.

––––––––– *NOTES* –––––––––

1. Andrew Billingsley, "Black Families in a Changing Society," in *The State of Black America 1987*, ed., Janet Dewart (New York: The National Urban League, Inc.), pp. 99-100.

2. Sharon Robinson, *Taking Charge: An Approach to Making the Educational Problems of Blacks Comprehensible and Manageable*, in J. Dewart, p. 33.

3. The Congress of National Black Churches includes the following denominations: African Methodist Episcopal (AME), Christian Methodist Episcopal (CME), Church of God in Christ (COGIC), the National Baptist Convention of America, and the Progressive National Baptist Baptist Convention.

4. See Alex Poinsett, "Suffering the Little Children," *Ebony* (August 1988), pp. 144-48.

5. See for example, David Thompson, *A Black Elite* (New York: Greenwood Press, 1986).

6. William Julius Wilson, *The Truly Disadvantaged* (Chicago: University of Chicago, 1987).

7. Billingsley, p. 108.

8. *Ibid.*, pp. 105-06.

9. This position is central to Wilson's argument in *The Truly Disadvantaged*.

10. Billingsley, p. 109.

11. Theo. Witvliet, *The Way of the Black Church*, trans by J. Bowden (Oak Park, Ill.: Meyer Stone Books, 1987), p. 214.

12. James M. Burns, *Leadership* (New York: Harper and Row, 1978), p. 19.

13. *Ibid.*, p. 18.

14. *Ibid.*, p. 20.

15. *Ibid.*, pp. 19-20.

16. Hans Van der Bent, *From Generation to Generation* (Geneva: World Council of Churches, 1986), p. 107.

17. *Ibid.*, p. 108.

18. *Ibid.*

19. Michael Warren, *Youth, Gospel, Liberation* (New York: Harper and Row, 1987), p. 40.

20. *Ibid.*

21. *Ibid.*

22. Erik Erikson, *Identity and the Life Cycle* (New York: International Universities Press, 1959), p. 65.

23. James Fowler, *Stages of Faith* (San Francisco: Harper and Row, 1981), p. 122 ff.

24. Sally McFague, *Models of God* (Philadelphia: Fortress Press, 1987), p. 33.

25. Kosuke Koyama, "The Ecumenical Movement as the Dialogue of Cultures," *Faith and Faithfulness*, ed., Paula Webb, (Geneva: World Council of Churches, 1984), p. 41.

26. Charles Gerkin, *Widening the Horizons* (Philadelphia: Westminster Press, 1986), p. 61.

CHAPTER FIVE

Elements of a
Black Youth Ministry

CHARLES R. FOSTER

*T*he task of this chapter is to identify and describe major elements in the church's ministry to black youth. Only recently churches have asked if there is anything distinctive about black youth ministry. An affirmative response to that question establishes the framework for this final chapter. We contend that both purposes and approaches to black youth ministry emerge from the dialogue of the African American Christian religious heritage and the contemporary experience of black youth. The previous chapters set that dialogue in motion.

Radical changes occurring in the relationship of black churches to the larger community and of black youth to the church lend a sense of urgency to the discussion of the purposes and organization of black youth ministry. Adolescents are especially vulnerable to the impact of major social changes. They stand at the threshold of assuming adult roles and responsibilities in the community. They increasingly make personal decisions about the optional values and ideals they encounter—including those affecting the relationship of personal identity and religious faith. The complexity of the tasks they face on the threshold of adulthood is heightened by the increasing pluralism in the religious and social experience in the African American community.

No longer is it possible, for example, to identify the African American religious experience with Christianity, as most interpreters of the black church have done. The growth of Muslim and pan-African religious movements has introduced to many urban people a wider range of options for faith commitments than those offered by major black Christian churches. Neither can it be assumed that black youth will identify with various religious movements in the African American tradition.

An increasing number of African American young people now participate in predominantly white Christian congregations. Indeed it cannot be assumed that African American youth will identify with the faith concerns and life styles of any traditional religious community. An increasing number simply no longer participate in the life of any faith community.

Demographic changes also challenge traditional church approaches to black youth. The immigration of peoples from the Caribbean, Latin America, and Africa continue to enrich and diversify the African American community. The mass movement of black Americans during the depression, World War II, and from the civil rights era to the present further diversified the black cultural and religious experience. The cultural and geographical influence of the west coast, the northern industrial cities, the urban and rural south have contributed to the increasingly multi-valent character of African American cultural experience. Integrated schools and neighborhoods (even with their limitations) have increased the options available to many black youth. The expansion of these options has also contributed to the disruption of the homogeneity of black cultural values and the continuity of African American social relationships and structures.

One of the most obvious potential problems created by these new possibilities has been described earlier by Moseley: the increasing disparity between those black youth who are moving out into the larger culture of the nation and those left behind economically in ghettos of poverty. Churches, consequently, can no longer assume homogeneity in the cultural experience of black youth.

A third challenge to traditional approaches to black youth ministry comes from the intrusion of the values of the media, consumer, and drug cultures into their homes and communities. There is no way for churches to protect youth from daily encountering these values. They permeate to varying degrees almost every sector of the larger community. They present youth with negative value systems that stand over against the traditional values of church, school, and family. Youth are especially vulnerable to these forces in our midst because, as Michael Warren has observed, they erode and fragment the values that unify and nurture the common life.[1] The pervasiveness of their influence, however, means the church can no longer assume that black youth are motivated by the visions and values of the religious heritage of African Americans.

Ministries to youth in general, and to black youth in particular, cannot be taken for granted. If the church is committed to the formative power of the gospel into the next generation, a systematic and concerted ministry approach to its youth becomes imperative. The preceding chapters provide several clues to the shape of such a ministry. In the pages that follow we will attempt to identify those elements and explore their implications for the organization of ministries with black youth.

Purpose of Black Youth Ministry

A primary purpose for black youth ministry is to call youth into discipleship. This purpose embodies the identity and vocation central to the experience of adolescence. Identity has to do with allegiance and commitment—"whose am I?" It involves two interdependent tasks. From a Christian perspective the first involves clarifying one's relationship to Jesus Christ and the community formed in loyalty through history to Christ. In this regard black youth ministry is similar to any youth ministry.

In the second task, however, identity involves clarifying one's relationship to the meanings and experiences of one's cultural heritage—in this case, the heritage of African Americans. The two tasks are interdependent because the call of Christ always comes through the experiences of people in particular cultural and historical communities. It is couched in the symbols and patterns that give vitality and meaning to those communities. It is out of the history and in the midst of the African American experience, that the significance and power of Christ's call has been made manifest to black Christians in the United States.

This is what Grant means when she states theology is grounded in African American experience. It is what Moseley means when he emphasizes that the church's ministry to youth requires sustaining youth (in and through their families) in the deep structure or grammar of faith. That structure or grammar is couched in the relationship of Christ to his disciples in specific languages and symbols that speak to people living in concrete times and places. It bears the imprint of his character but is heard and seen through distinctively cultural patterns and modes. In the interplay of call and commitment to Christ heard and responded to through the medium of the African American experience the identity of black youth takes form.

Vocation has to do with the embodiment or expression of that commitment to Christ in the community for the sake of the life of the community. Vocation reveals the depth of the response of people to the call of Christ in service to the community as an agent of Christ. As such it is a political activity, as Moseley reminds us, engaging the values and ideals of Christ shaped in the crucible of the black experience for the sake of that community and the welfare of all humankind. Discipleship is consequently both the aim and the means of black youth ministry.

The emphasis upon discipleship in black youth ministry avoids the confusion in many churches over whether to view youth as the church of tomorrow or as participants in the church's ministry today. The call to discipleship is lifelong. It may begin through some profound conversion experience. But it can be sustained only through the continuing nurture of the commitment people make in and through transformational encounters with the presence of Christ. Both new disciples and old disciples are disciples. Hence this intergenerational task of ministry must nurture commitment to Christ and service to neighbor in all disciples. Moreover, congregations *must* assess the extent to which their ministries to youth intensify their commitment to Christ and help develop their sense of responsibility to be the agents of Christ's ministry through their adolescent years.

This goal for youth ministry in Grant's words, centers on nurturing a sense of somebodiness in youth. To be somebody means that a person has a sense of clarity about him or herself—*"I am somebody."* To be somebody means giving significance to others—*"you are somebody."* To be somebody also means a person is acclaimed for contributing to the welfare of others— *"you have made me (us) somebody."* To be somebody is to maintain increasing clarity through the tasks of identity and vocation—to be human, even to the fullness of the humanity that was in Christ.

Several implications may be found in a youth ministry emphasis upon nurturing somebodiness. It will be *evangelical.* When youth are confronted with many options for their commitments, churches are faced with the task of presenting the gospel of Jesus Christ in a way that makes it relevant to their experience. The diminishing involvement of black youth in church life underscores the importance of church's reaching out to where youth are. But the evangelical character of youth ministry is even more evident in the extent to which the teaching, worship, social witness, and fellowship of congregations actually influences their futures.

The call to discipleship must reveal the viability of the gospel for their lives. For these youth the church must be more than a lively repository of the black cultural heritage. It must be engaged in the contemporary task of responding to God's call to faithfulness in the face of the issues and problems these young men and women face. This is what Moseley means when he calls for a ministry that will help youth make sense out of the paradox of the suffering of the black experience and the liberation of the gospel.

The viability of the gospel is most evident in ministries that are *hope-filled.* Especially for black youth trapped in cycles of poverty and frustration, the call to discipleship is essentially a call to hope in the face of what often appears to be absolute hopelessness. Grant, Moseley, and

Hale-Benson have each documented different dimensions of the conditions for hopelessness among black youth. A gospel of other worldly escape does not serve these youth well. It may nurture the identity of youth in Christ, but it does not engage youth in the possibility that they might embody that relationship through the development of their own gifts and graces for ministry.

A black youth ministry concerned with nurturing "somebodiness" will be evangelical, hope-filled, and *liberating*. Despite the political and economic advances of parts of the black community since the civil rights movement, all black youth continue to encounter the residue of racism in blatant as well as carefully disguised forms. Consequently, the call to discipleship continues to come as a call to liberation. Liberation is experienced as respect—a sign of God's trust in our human capacity to be agents of justice and hope. Liberation is experienced as dignity—a tribute to the creativeness of God found in the diversity of our gifts and graces for ministry. Liberation is experienced as freedom—bounded not by the strictures of human agency, but by the vastness of God's grace. Liberation is also experienced as responsibility, the extension of God's liberating love for others. Liberation, in other words, is basic to the adolescent quest for identity and vocation.

The Congregation as Agent of Youth Ministry

Nicholas C. Cooper-Lewter and Henry H. Mitchell in *Soul Theology* have claimed that one of the core beliefs of African American peoples is "that they are all related as a family." This belief system emphasizing the basic kinship of all people "presumes folk to be related and obligated to each other until proven otherwise." Cooper-Lewter and Mitchell observe that this commitment is evident in the way black churches function, even though few tend to use the doctrine of the church as the family of God in describing themselves.[2]

The ideal of the church as the family of God draws heavily upon both biblical and African traditions. It emphasizes the view of the ancient Akan and Ashanti proverb: "Because we are, I am." And it acknowledges the profound Hebrew insight that one's future is found in one's children. The church as the family of God is what a number of educators would now call an intergenerational community. Moseley reminds us that this means people are bound together across the generations. They are gathered into *oikumene*, that household of God encompassing all persons. This interdependence across the generations both invites participation in the whole and presumes a mutuality of responsibility for each other.

It is this latter point that is so crucial today. If churches take the religious and cultural heritage of black youth seriously, adolescents are seen as an integral part of the family, the congregation, the community, and the world. They are inextricably bound up in living out of the visions each of these social entities has of its own future. They are the bearers of its heritage. They participate in the mutuality of its sense of responsibility for each other and all persons. This process generates what Moseley calls intergenerational faith. The faith of the elderly informs the experience of the young. The experience of the young revitalizes and transforms the faith of their elders for new circumstances and situations. It is a historic, communal, and family faith, received and renewed at the same time in profoundly personal ways.

The black church serves as that community of persons

which embodies the intensification of the African American Christian religious experience through time. Our use of the word "intensification" is intentional. It is a technical word drawn from research into the ritual processes of communities. It illuminates how the primary corporate actions in the life of a community contribute to the continuity and renewal of community life. That is why Hale-Benson emphasizes the importance of identifying and using traditional African American cultural patterns in the education of black youth.

In black churches worship and education, mission and other primary community events channel the efforts of people to articulate the traditions and contemporary experiences of black peoples through the symbols of Christian faith. It rehearses the interplay of African American and biblical stories. It reviews the experience of daily living and gathers the community as the family of God into the mutuality of corporate confession, grief, celebration, and praise. It politicizes and energizes itself for living into the week. It renews the bonds of congregational identity and faithfulness. And it sets the stage for youth to converse with people in the larger community and around the world about issues of faith and life that affect their futures.

Three Tasks of Black Youth Ministry

Just as cultures and communities vary, so do congregational approaches to youth ministry. William Myers, an advocate for youth and an interpreter of youth ministry, has described in a still unpublished book one black church youth ministry organized around the youth leadership of the fifth Sunday service of worship.[3] An increasingly popular form of black youth ministry occurs through the youth gospel choir. Many small churches do not have enough youth to create a separate age level ministry. So they integrate the youth who are present into the full life of the congregation. The youth serve as Sunday school teachers, sing in the choir, work as ushers, help out with special mission and fellowship activities of the church; and, in some cases, they even serve as congregational officers. Some of the most effective youth ministries involve the cooperation of several congregations—often across denominational lines. Project Image directed to the needs of young black men and Project Pride to the needs of young black women in Chicago are illustrative.[4]

Some black youth ministries are based in the congregation, some in the neighborhood, and others in the total community. Some youth ministries are directed to youth of the church and others to youth outside the church. No one form or approach to black youth ministry is definitive. Each has the potential to call youth into discipleship. Consequently the forms and structures of black youth ministry may vary, but they all share at least three tasks integral to the call of youth into discipleship.

1. *Black youth ministry involves incorporating or binding youth into the life and mission of the church as the contemporary extension and expression of Christ's ministry.* Moseley calls this task both the retrieval of intergenerational faith and the building up of the household of God. His point is that the continuity of the community of faith shaped by the gospel through the African American experience depends upon the effectiveness of congregations to gather youth into the historic faith traditions of African American Christians. The heritage of any people continues to have power only if subsequent generations find in it the resources to live with meaning into the issues they face in daily life. Moseley also observes that the black youth's Christian identity depends upon this task. The processes of binding the generations is a cultural and religious necessity for both the continuity of the community and the identity of individual persons. Specifically, the somebodiness of black youth is rooted in the discovery of their personhood within the family context of the African American heritage.

In an intergenerational community of faith, discipleship in its most profound sense is a relational matter. Its meanings and responsibilities are deeply rooted in both biblical and African imagery of God's reconciling grace. These images give distinctive meaning and power to the sense of personal worth and social responsibility. God unconditionally accepts. This theme persisted in the attention to the study of scripture and the exposition of biblical themes in the spirituals and preaching of African American churches for generations. In the act of God's acceptance people discover they are unique in God's sight, but the experience of uniqueness is one shared with all of God's children. God's acceptance involves an intensely personal realization of both one's own identity and that of the larger community.

The pluralistic character of black youth culture and experience means that the binding of youth into the African American Christian experience can no longer be assumed. Therefore, black youth ministries must necessarily focus upon self-conscious and intentional efforts to incorporate black youth into a life style of discipleship. That process begins in the efforts of congregations to help youth become so familiar with the stories, symbols, and traditions of the African American Christian experience that they become the means for understanding and articulating their identities and responsibilities as African American Christians.

E. D. Hirsch, Jr. stresses the basic importance of this task in his reminder that no community can continue to exist if its members do not share the stories, symbols, and traditions of their common identity and heritage *and* the information represented by those symbols.[5] That information, crucial to communication with each other, is essential to the continuity of the community's sense of identity and purpose.

No wonder then, that Grant challenges the use of curriculum resources in the church which deny black youth the opportunity to appropriate their religious and cultural heritage through African American Christian perspectives. No wonder then that she calls for the institution of black religious studies in churches in which black youth might be immersed in the shared symbols and meanings of the African American Christian experience. No wonder that Hale-Benson emphasizes an approach to teaching and learning that embodies the expectations of that cultural heritage. Moseley points to the character of these efforts in his proposal that black youth ministry be organized in part, around the ministries of the word and worship because historically, these two ministries have distinctively unified and grounded the corporate identity of the African American Christian community.

The intergenerational character of the task to bind youth into the life and mission of Christ's ministry influences the way churches share community stories, symbols, and traditions. The process is more than a transmissive one. The black religious experience is participatory and communal. Everyone belongs-across the age spectrum. Each person has a place and a potential contribution. Therefore the task of appropriating the symbols that identify one with the symbols and "core beliefs" of African American Christians necessitates the full participation of youth in the church's life and mission.

The process is familiar. A young person is asked to read the scripture in worship. An adult who cares both for the young person and the quality of worship as an act of community praise and thanksgiving supervises the young person in the practice of the public reading of scripture. After the worship service, many adults from the congregation surround the young person to congratulate, affirm, and to offer suggestions. This process has traditionally occurred in many churches through the contribution of youth to music and worship leadership, the supervision of younger children by youth, the inclusion of youth in community projects that care for people with special needs.

The central role youth played in protest and resistance during the civil rights movement may illustrate the wider range of possibilities for youth ministry. Their ability to bear the brunt of the effort to integrate schools, restaurants, and other places of public accommodation witnesses to the potential for social transformation in their faith. Their sensitivity to the need they experienced for support and encouragement reveals the depths of their compassion. Their ability to approach crisis-ridden situations with clarity of mind and conviction illustrates their maturity potential. Their contribution to the movement cannot be underestimated. Neither can the potential of their contribution to the life and mission of the church in the local community or the world at large.

The intergenerational structure of youth participation may be discerned in the example above. Youth (whether they volunteered, were selected by their peers, or chosen by adults) assume a visible and contributing role to the larger community. They are then trained to fulfill that role to the glory of God, the pleasure, and the welfare of the community. They assume responsibility for designated tasks or roles. Their contribution is assessed and they are affirmed—an act which intensifies both the bonds of the community and the sense of self-esteem and purpose crucial to the nurture of identity and vocation.

The binding of youth into the community of faith in other words, involves transmitting those stories, symbols, and traditions that distinguish the life and mission of the community; training youth to participate in the church's mission in the larger community; and nurturing relationships with significant adults who envision in those same youth the future of the community and who model for them what it means to live as disciples.

2. *Black youth ministry involves advocating for black youth a viable future.* It draws upon the historic emphasis upon the liberation of the oppressed in the African American Christian experience. Advocacy ministries provide the basis for any ministry truly engaged in the kind of healing Moseley calls for. The advocacy of a future for youth takes many forms. One of the most obvious examples is seen in the long-term commitment of black churches to the education of children and youth. Many black colleges and schools have their origins in the decisions of congregations in the last century to ensure for their young people an education—usually at great personal and corporate sacrifice.

Much of the impetus to the integration of schools during the fifties and sixties came from the leadership and membership of black churches concerned about the nature of the education of black children and youth. In recent years this same concern is often most evident in church-sponsored programs to make sure that the futures of today's children and youth will not be hindered by inadequate schooling. These new programs range from after school tutorials, to Saturday schools, to alternative schools.[6]

Another example is found in the efforts of church and community leaders who raise to public consciousness the plight of contemporary youth—especially those who are trapped in cycles of poverty, bad education, inadequate housing, and fragmented communities. These problems visibly and irretrievably limit the futures of youth. They block or at least impede the exercise and development of the gifts and graces bestowed by God on youth.

In less visible ways, however, all youth are victimized in the current economic and political struggles over the distribution of available resources. Communities across the nation consistently make choices affecting youth. Some of the most obvious may be seen in the seeming preference of communities for prisons rather than crime prevention or rehabilitation programs, lower taxes rather than quality schools, roads rather than parks or playgrounds, or medical programs that feature the heroic rather than the everyday needs of families. In these struggles youth have little experience or power to advocate for themselves in the larger social and economic circles of contemporary life.

Even more, they lack the power to influence significantly the political, economic, and educational systems that contribute to their present oppression and deny to them a viable future. Youth need people who will speak for them in the competition for the limited resources available in our society. The task involves speaking for them when they have no voice, representing them when they have little influence, as well as training them to speak and to represent themselves when and where that might be possible.

Ministries of advocacy depend upon an accurate understanding of the situations in which black youth find themselves. Consequently their effectiveness requires the systematic and intentional analysis of the institutional and systemic sources of oppression, discrimination, and racism affecting youth. The essays in this volume identify the general sources and character of those forces in the experience of youth. They are experienced however, in very specific situations and places. Knowing something about racism, poverty, or age discrimination in general, does not provide appropriate data to develop strategies for the liberation of specific groups of people. The task confronting churches concerned about black youth has to do with identifying and naming the specific sources of the oppression of the youth they serve. This step makes possible the development of appropriate strategies to equip youth to combat the forces limiting their futures.

Gwendolyn Rice, Director of Project Image in a recent article, illustrates the movement from the analysis of the situation of youth to program development. She points out that Project Image is concerned with the facts that in Chicago the school dropout rate of black males 16 years of age and over runs around 70%; the unemployment of black youth ranges from 46% to 52%. Homicide is the primary source of death among black male youth, and that one of six black males will be arrested before he reaches[19]. Project Image in other words, begins with a reading of the situation of urban youth. It makes use of studies to name the impediments to a viable future for young black men. The challenge for Project Image consequently has been to develop a program or strategy to nurture young men toward successful adulthood—a phrase that encompasses a sense of self-worth and the sense of responsibility for others.[7]

The strategy of Project Image is *church based* because churches are located in the midst of the neighborhoods where youth are found. Black churches have historically functioned as neighborhood centers. Black churches moreover, have the inherited ability to provide the sense of family we discussed earlier that is missing for vast numbers of urban poor youth. This program is *ecumenical* because the problem is larger than the resources of any one congregation. Its effectiveness hinges on the *relationship* of the community's strong, effective black male leaders to black young men. Its program is *comprehensive* in that it involves black youth in personal relationships with adults in ways that introduce to them new ways of viewing themselves through sports activities, the support of effective school habits, and successful employment. It includes instruction in the content of the Christian and African American traditions, thereby providing youth with a heritage filled with symbols that have the capacity to empower them for the problems and possibilities they face.[8] If participants had access to the discussion of these issues from a global perspective as Moseley suggests, the program would take on an *intercultural* dimension as well.

A ministry of advocacy however, does not end with either analysis or programs to provide youth with coping skills. It must ultimately involve an encounter with the institutional structures of government, industry, business, and the church at the points where the futures of black youth are most clearly inhibited. The involvement of church leaders in the movement to desegregate schools provides one example of an advocacy ministry that led to systematic changes. Similar efforts are needed to alter the conditions contributing to the unemployment, drug use, teenage pregnancy, ineffective schooling, and problems of self-esteem among many young people.

A ministry advocating a viable future for black youth consequently includes adults who speak out and negotiate for youth at the points of their powerlessness. It also encompasses ministries that equip youth with the skills to influence their own futures. It also engages in political and legal activities to improve the systemic conditions for the creation of a viable future for youth.

3. *Black youth ministry involves training youth for leadership in Christ's ministry.* At this point we confront a typical misunderstanding in the way people view discipleship. It has little to do with nurturing in people passive emulation of some great figure—even Jesus. Instead it emphasizes the kind of training in the teachings and life style of the master that culminates in the liberation of disciples. The transformational character of this process may be traced to Peter as he changed from the awestruck and awkward fisherman into the powerful leader of the early church under the influence of Jesus. Discipleship in this sense is the activity of the empowered for the sake of the powerless that they too might be empowered for ministries of service.

Moseley introduced a new theme into his discussion on the importance of training black youth for leadership.[9] He calls for developing in youth the ability to be transforming leaders—a form of leadership that makes a difference in our churches and communities because it is grounded in the relationship of leaders to Jesus Christ (the source of their identity and vocation) and because it engages leaders in liberating activities out of the traditions and resources of the African American Christian heritage.

Transforming leadership has four elements. Each calls for a specific response from congregations seeking to nurture that ability in its youth. The first response of transforming leadership is located in the relationship of young people to Jesus Christ. In that relationship the somebodiness of a person is determined by the grace of God rather than the structures of society. It means that the source of one's identity and vocation transcends the expectations of those around us. It ensures our freedom to walk around the structures of society in much the same way Daniel wandered around the lion's den. It means we view the events and circumstances of the world from God's perspective rather than from a human perspective. It reminds us that the impetus of leadership comes not from some quest for status, power, or prestige on our part, but from God's desire for justice in all of creation. It enables us to discern the oppressive and demonic features in our own cultural heritage and communities. Transforming leadership is grounded in the quality and depth of our commitments to Jesus Christ. As participants in the community of faith, youth have already been invited to be leaders in Christ's transforming ministry.

Transforming leadership draws upon a vision for a group or situation that transcends the immediacy of the experience of the people involved. This second characteristic articulates a unifying sense of the future that pulls a community toward and into it. Vision is crucial to the continuity of a community. This point has recently been made by Warren Bennis and Burt Nanus, prominent students of leadership theory. They conclude that the capacity to envision new possibilities distinguishes effective from ineffective leaders because they draw upon the "emotional and spiritual resources" of the community.[10]

The resources to envision are deeply rooted in the African American Christian experience. Slaves appropriated the promises of liberation experienced in the Exodus and in the freedom of the early church faith in the resurrection of Christ. Both the Exodus and the resurrection of Christ served as symbols for their own liberation and freedom. Those stories and symbols took root in their own immediate experience. They inspired, motivated, and guided the actions of countless men and women through years of servitude and bondage.

The task of visioning for contemporary African American Christians contrasts with that of their ancestors. The forms of oppression are more subtle. The structures of bondage are more complex. The dangers for all humanity are more comprehensive. Youth live into a future with growing disparity between those who have and those who have not. They will not be assured of jobs in our rapidly changing world unless they have the ability to adjust to changing technologies and institutional structures. They are faced with the threat of fragmenting communities, an environment so polluted as to be dangerous to their health and welfare, and the spectre of nuclear annihilation—all with little regard to any particular cultural heritage or identity. The future for youth is a fragile one. It could easily become a hopeless future. It therefore becomes essential for the sake of all humanity that youth ministry provide practice in envisioning in the face of these forces. That effort will necessarily involve training youth to discern in the visions of their African American Christian heritage, clues to the issues and problems all of humanity faces in our own time.

A third element of transforming leadership involves the ability to act with meaning and power in more than one cultural milieu—a crucial skill if black youth are to help give direction to the future of a pluralistic society. From one perspective black youth generally are at an advantage in this regard. To be African American has meant learning to appropriate ways of seeing, acting, and relating from at least two cultures. But the ability to make use of the resources and customs of their experience of living in more than one culture has also been a negative experience for African Americans. As W. E. B. Du Bois pointed out years ago, the traditional relationships of European Americans and African Americans had little to do with a reciprocity of respect or the equivalence of influence. To be an African American meant seeing oneself through the cultural judgment of European Americans. The resulting double consciousness robbed African American men and women of their dignity and the larger society of the richness of African American perspectives on common issues and concerns.

The increasing pluralism of the nation however, provides a powerful opportunity to cast off the hierarchical character of cross-cultural communication and to retrieve for our own church and national life something of the mutuality of cultures originating from all parts of the globe to be found in the experience of Pentecost. Just as significant for this new pattern of social relationships is the potential found in the global ecumenical conversations among youth for discovering how to discern and respond to God's liberating activity from more than one cultural perspective.

This task is crucial to the liberation that is central to transforming leadership. It begins with the development of a clear understanding of one's own cultural heritage and identity. Neither the gospel or the power structures of the world are culturally neutral. Their capacity to empower and to transform occurs through the ability of leaders to draw upon the deepest of specific cultural symbols and to discern in them possibilities for all humankind. The resources of the African American Christian heritage consequently only have the potential to be of continuing service to humanity when youth selfconsciously begin to use them in and through their own work.

At the same time transforming leaders in multicultural societies must develop both an understanding of the heritage, values, and commitments and a proficiency in the skills of another culture(s) to participate in that culture unselfconsciously. This process is most familiar to us in foreign language study—especially in those experiences where children or youth participate in an intensive encounter with the language, food, and customs of the people being studied. This kind of education provides youth with the ability to participate in the church's larger mission in the nation and around the world.

Transforming leadership further depends upon the capacity of people to view both their own cultural heritage and identity and that of others from a transcendent perspective. This means youth have the capacity to recognize the finitude of any culture or societal structure. This is evident in their sensitivity to the hypocrisy of adults, churches, and other value oriented institutions. They also have the increasing ability to discern points of commonality in and through the contrasting symbol systems of various cultural communities. But it takes practice to translate those insights into the actions that will help churches and communities be faithful to the leadership of Christ in and for our own time and situation.

A final element in transforming leadership happens to be the most familiar in discussions on leadership. It involves the explicit training of youth in practicing skills central to the activity of what Moseley has called transactional leadership. This is the leadership crucial to the tasks of initiating ideas and programs, negotiating options, exercising power to implement decisions, mobilizing people, and promoting common values and concerns. Again black churches have a long history of helping youth work on many of these skills—public speaking and reading, parliamentary procedure, and attention to the interpersonal dynamics of leadership.

In the complexity of our modern world however, these skills alone are insufficient to the task of training transforming leaders. It is just as important to help youth develop skills to function effectively in and through the institutions that give form and continuity to modern day living. These organizational skills include the ability to discern patterns of power and authority, recruit volunteers, identify the needs of people and programs, set goals, develop strategies to accomplish those goals, and to evaluate the consequences of their efforts and the faithfulness of their participation in the ministry of Christ. Contemporary leaders must deal with both people and institutional structures that often seem to function without attending to the people who make them up. Transforming leaders have the knowledge and skills to function in both arenas.

These transactional leadership skills have the potential to contribute to transforming leadership especially when they are accompanied by the ability to understand and interpret the meanings of the events in which people find themselves. Youth therefore need to develop the skills for articulating those meanings out of the stories, symbols, and traditions of the African American Christian heritage. This interpretive task brings into focus the continuity of the meanings of their experience from the past. It means they begin helping people find power in their own heritage. It also helps them to name the implications of their experience for the future. In that act they begin to help people discover meaning and hope in their experience. They become agents in God's liberating activity.

Summary

Perhaps the most useful way to summarize our conclusions for the future directions of black youth ministry would be to identify a set of questions that might guide the work of church leaders with youth. They may be used to evaluate existing ministries or to plan new ministries. It is our expectation that most of the questions that follow will be useful to the leadership of congregations, ecumenical groups, denominational agencies, and curriculum editors.

A GUIDE TO EVALUATING AND PLANNING BLACK YOUTH MINISTRIES

1. What purposes guide your approach to ministries involving black youth?

    A. Do these purposes clearly articulate that the sources for the identity and vocation of black youth involves clarifying their relationship both to Jesus Christ and to their own cultural history?

    B. Do these puposes reflect the historic role of scripture in binding the black community together as it faces the contemporary world.

    C. Do they promote a sense of somebodiness in theological, personal, and social dimensions?

    D. Are the purposes relevant enough to the experience of the youth you serve that they will take your invitation to participate seriously? Do they provide for active youth engagement in ministries of love and justice?

   E. Do the purposes convey a sense of hope?
   F. Will they help youth experience the liberation that undergirds both personal and social freedom and responsibility?

2. What forces in your congregation or setting will help build a strong ministry for black youth? What forces will inhibit the development of a strong ministry? (Look at attitudes, other priorities of the congregation or group, the commitments, skills, and interest of adult leaders, the availability of useful space, financial resources, external forces and pressures, etc.) What forces in your congregation or setting will help or hinder the development of a youth ministry that is both intergenerational and includes people from a wide range of socio-economic backgrounds?

3. In what ways is the youth ministry directed toward helping youth develop the understandings and skills to be effective leaders in ministry?

   A. How will youth develop significant relationships with adults who both model patterns of discipleship and intergenerational mutuality?
   B. How are youth welcomed or discouraged from participating in congregational life?
   C. How will youth participate in ecumenical, denominational, and global conversations around the issues affecting the development of their own sense of somebodiness as disciples of Jesus Christ?
   D. How are youth engaged in studying the scriptures and traditions of the African American Christian experience? What curricular resources are needed for such a program of studies? How useful are those resources which are available? What might you need to develop?

E. What contributions can youth make to the worship, mission, education, and fellowship of the congregation, ecumenical group, or denomination?

F. What specifically blocks a viable future for the youth you serve? What programs or agencies are currently attempting to address these "blocks"? How effective are they? What other programs need to be established to help youth in their quest for a viable future?

G. In what ways is the relationship of youth to Jesus Christ explicitly nurtured through this program of ministry?

H. Where in the ministry of the church do youth encounter and explore the visions that have given hope to African American Christians in the past? In what ways do they participate in the church's efforts to envision a viable and faithful future now?

I. How and where do black youth have the opportunity to reflect on their experiences in other cultural settings in ways that help them to function more effectively in them? In what ways are they encouraged to develop skills to participate in other cultural contexts without denying or inhibiting their own heritage?

J. What opportunities for leadership training in groups, organizations, and institutions are provided youth through your ministry (public speaking, planning procedures, decision making skills, recruiting and training skills, etc.)?

——————— *NOTES* ———————

1. Michael Warren, *Youth, Gospel, Liberation* (San Francisco: Harper and Row, 1987), p. 53.

2. Nicholas C. Cooper-Lewter and Henry H. Mitchell, *Soul Theology: The Heart of American Black Culture* (San Francisco: Harper and Row, 1986), pp. 127-28.

3. William R. Myers of Chicago Theological Seminary has described the work of a black youth ministry in an unpublished paper entitled "Black and White Styles of Youth Ministry", 1987.

4. For a description of Project Image see Gwendolyn Rice, "Young Black Men, the Church, and Our Future," *The Chicago Theological Seminary Register.* (Spring 1988), # 2, pp. 10-15.

5. E. D. Hirsch, Jr., *Cultural Literacy: What Every American Should Know* (New York: Vintage Books, 1988), p. xvii.

6. For a description of a recent effort to safeguard the education of children see Alex Poinsett, "Reflections on People: Empowering Stewardship," *The Chicago Theological Seminary Register*, pp. 6-7.

7. Rice, p. 11.

8. Rice, pp. 13-15.

9. In this regard Moseley refers to the work of Warren Bennis and Burt Nanus, two prominent interpreters of leadership theory. In their most recent work, they call for a "new" theory of leadership which centers on "organizational transformation to ensure long-term vitality." They call this approach "transformative leadership." Warren Bennis and Burt Nanus, *Leaders: The Strategies for Taking Charge* (New York: Harper and Row, 1985), p. 3.

10. *Ibid.*, pp. 89-92.